LEADER-
COACH

LEADER-COACH

DEVELOPING EFFECTIVE MINISTRY TEAMS

STAN TOLER & LARRY GILBERT

BEACON HILL PRESS
OF KANSAS CITY

Library of Congress Cataloging-in-Publication Data

Toler, Stan.
  Leader-coach : developing effective ministry teams / Stan Toler, Larry Gilbert.
    pages cm
  Includes bibliographical references.
  ISBN 978-0-8341-2940-5 (pbk.)
  1. Christian leadership. 2. Church work. I. Title.
  BV652.1.T6455 2013
  253—dc23

                                                    2012049199

10 9 8 7 6 5 4 3 2 1

CONTENTS

▲

ACKNOWLEDGMENTS

▲

Thanks to Bonnie Perry, Deloris Leonard, Pat Diamond, Cathy Buchanan, Larry Wilson, Barry Russell, Judi Perry, and the entire team at Beacon Hill Press of Kansas City.

RESOURCE TIPS

▲

Improving your ministry by creating effective Ministry Action Teams is the subject of this book, and there are other resources you can use to help implement the concepts taught here. Watch for the Resource Tip section at the conclusion of each chapter, which provides a cross link to other helpful materials. Keep your growth journey going—even after you finish this book.

PREFACE

▲

Basketball great Michael Jordan once scored a remarkable sixty-four points in a game against the Orlando Magic, but his team lost the game anyway. Even though Michael's scoring ability and dazzling acrobatics made him an instant superstar, he was in the National Basketball Association for six seasons before his team attained a championship. Jordan discovered that it wasn't very satisfying to be a superstar on a losing team. Being the NBA Rookie of the Year in 1985 was wonderful, and it was quite an achievement to be the top scorer in the league for seven consecutive seasons beginning in 1987, but Michael longed for an NBA championship.

He had to learn to direct his sensational abilities toward helping his team win rather than merely scoring a lot of points. When he began to devote himself to teamwork—helping each of his teammates reach his full potential—the results were dramatic. Before his retirement from the game in 1999, Michael led the Chicago Bulls to six NBA championships.

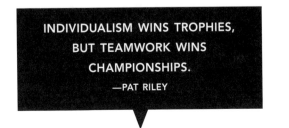

INDIVIDUALISM WINS TROPHIES,
BUT TEAMWORK WINS
CHAMPIONSHIPS.

—PAT RILEY

Church leaders need to learn the same lesson. Rather than striving for personal "stardom," they need to develop ministry teams within their churches. The team concept is the foundational strategy for effective ministry in a local church.

The apostle Paul acknowledged that his ministry accomplishments were achieved with the help of many other people. Their love, encouragement, prayers, and financial support were indispensable to his success. (See 2 Corinthians 1:11; 1 Corinthians 16:17–18; Romans 16:1–6; and Philippians 2:17–30.) He didn't consider the people in his churches to be his *audience* but rather his *fellow workers* (2 Corinthians 1:24).

Paul, like Michael Jordan, was so gifted that he undoubtedly was tempted to go it alone. The great apostle and the famous basketball player weren't in the same league—literally or figuratively—but they both understood that working together with others was the key to maximum success. They knew that the way to victory was found more in their "assists"—providing others with opportunities to achieve—than in scoring their own points. They learned to see themselves not only as players but also as coaches who could bring out the gifts in their teammates.

> ## THE MAIN INGREDIENT IN STARDOM IS THE REST OF THE TEAM.
> —JOHN WOODEN

The Bible doesn't emphasize solo ministry as much as it does team ministry. Its pages are filled with stories of great collaborations: Moses and Aaron, Caleb and Joshua, Esther and Mordecai, Ezra and Nehemiah, Peter and John, Paul and Timothy, Barnabas and Mark. Even the Gospels are presented to us by a team: Matthew, Mark, Luke, and John. Jesus made teamwork a priority in His earthly ministry with His team of twelve.

Overworked church administrators can effectively utilize the skills of laypersons gifted by the Holy Spirit for ministry. Pastors can learn the dynamics of a Ministry Action Team philosophy that revolutionizes their local churches. Laypersons can gain insights into their own potential for leading their communities to Christ and for building His kingdom.

I pray that you can get the job done through gifted individuals who catch your vision for changing the world.

Discover the joys of working as a team for the glory of God.

1

BUILD MINISTRY ACTION TEAMS

TWO ARE BETTER THAN ONE, BECAUSE THEY HAVE A GOOD
REWARD FOR THEIR LABOR. FOR IF THEY FALL, ONE WILL LIFT
UP HIS COMPANION. BUT WOE TO HIM WHO IS ALONE
WHEN HE FALLS, FOR HE HAS NO ONE TO HELP HIM UP.
—ECCLESIASTES 4:9–10

▲

Churches should be much more than Sunday morning entertainment centers for lukewarm saints. They should be training centers where people learn to win the lost for Christ. They should be growing by adding souls to the kingdom. But statistics show that only twenty percent of our churches are growing at all, and fewer than five percent are growing by conversions rather than transfer. This appalling lack of tangible results must call us to our knees in prayer and then to our feet in action if the Church is to fulfill the Great Commission that our Lord entrusted to us. Failure to employ effective ministry teams could be a major cause.

Roberta Hestenes said in Fuller Theological Seminary's *The Pastor's Update*, "Many churches are structured for maintenance rather than for empowering ministry among all God's people. We must reexamine our structures so that the new can come into being while preserving the essentials of our faith."

Most pastors know in their hearts that they can't single-handedly win the lost. They know they must have the active participation of the entire church. Successful church leadership isn't about superstardom; it's about effective team-building. Dedicated pastors have suffered burnout because they never learned this principle. Trying to do the job alone, they ended up much like the bricklayer who wrote the following letter to an insurance company to explain his injuries:

Dear sir:

I am writing in response to your request for more information concerning block No. 11 on the insurance form, which asks for "Cause of Injuries," wherein I put "trying to do the job alone." You said you needed more information, so I trust the following will be sufficient.

I am a bricklayer by trade, and on the date of injuries I was working alone laying brick around the top of a four-story building, when suddenly I realized that I had about five hundred pounds of brick left over. Rather than carry the bricks down by hand, I decided to put them into a barrel and lower them by a pulley that was fastened to the top of the building. I secured the end of the rope at ground level and went up to the top of the building, loaded the brick into the barrel, and flung the barrel out with the bricks in it. I then went down and untied the rope, holding it securely to insure the slow descent of the barrel.

As you will note in block No. 6 of the insurance form, I weigh 145 pounds. Due to my shock at being jerked off the ground so swiftly, I lost my presence of mind and forgot to let go of the rope. Between the second and the third floors I met the barrel, coming down. This accounts for the bruises and lacerations on my upper body.

Upon regaining my presence of mind, I held tightly to the rope and proceeded rapidly up the side of the building, not stopping until my right hand was jammed into the pulley. This accounts for my broken thumb.

Despite the pain, I retained my presence of mind and held tightly to the rope. At approximately the same time, however, the barrel of bricks hit the ground and the bottom fell out of the barrel. Devoid of the weight of the bricks, the barrel now weighed about fifty pounds. I again refer you to block No. 6 and my weight.

As you would guess, I began a rapid descent. In the vicinity of the second floor, I met the empty barrel coming up. This explains the injuries to my legs and lower body. Slowed only slightly, I continued my descent, landing on the pile of bricks. Fortunately, my back was only sprained, and the internal injuries were minimal. I am sorry to report, however, that at this point I again lost my presence of mind and let go of the rope. As you can imagine, the empty barrel crashed down on top of me.

I trust that this answers your concern. Please know that I am finished "trying to do the job alone."

Yours sincerely

The bricklayer discovered the hard way what church leaders are learning: trying to do the job alone can be a hazardous enterprise.

WHY BUILD MINISTRY ACTION TEAMS?

A number of definitions have been offered for the concept of team ministry. Chuck Bowman often says, "A team is two or more people with two things in common: a shared goal and good communication." Jon Katzenbach and Douglas Smith provide more detail when they write, "A team is a small number of people with complementary skills who are committed to a common purpose, performance goals, and approach for which they hold themselves mutually accountable." R. Daniel Reeves puts it this way: "Team ministry is ownership and self-initiated vision in which members carry out plans they themselves have conceived or have had a part in conceptualizing." Basically, team ministry refers to a group of church leaders working together for the purpose of building God's kingdom. These Ministry Action Teams will be vital to the success of the church in this new century.

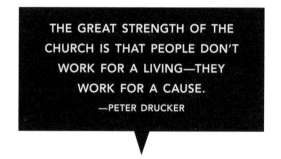

THE GREAT STRENGTH OF THE CHURCH IS THAT PEOPLE DON'T WORK FOR A LIVING—THEY WORK FOR A CAUSE.

—PETER DRUCKER

The key to understanding the value of Ministry Action Teams is found in the word "action." These teams exist so that something might be accomplished. Ministry Action Teams are characterized by three important traits.

1. Shared Vision and Values

A powerful synergy is created when leaders work together for common objectives: "Behold, how good and how pleasant it is for brethren to dwell together in unity. . . . For there the LORD commanded the blessing—Life forevermore" (Psalm 133:1, 3). Every Ministry Action Team needs to fully understand the church's mandate: "Go therefore and make disciples of all the nations, baptizing them in the name of the Father and of the Son and of the Holy Spirit, teaching them to observe all things that I have commanded you; and lo, I am with you always, even to the end of the age" (Matthew 28:19–20). And every church must fully understand that this primary goal given by our Lord cannot be achieved without a unity of purpose and an anointed team effort. In other words, the church must get its act together!

2. Biblical Models

Ministry is best performed in concert with other believers. The church must return to the biblical norm that so characterized the first-century Church: "So continuing daily with one accord in the temple, and breaking bread from house to house, they ate their food with gladness and simplicity of heart, praising God and having favor with all the people. And the Lord added to the church daily those who were being saved" (Acts 2:46–47).

Driven by rapid church growth, the Jerusalem church out of necessity adopted a team approach to meet the rising demands.

Now in those days, when the number of the disciples was multiplying, there arose a complaint against the Hebrews by the Hellenists, because their widows were neglected in the daily distribution. Then the twelve summoned the multitude of the disciples and said, "It is not desirable that we should leave the word of God and serve tables. Therefore, brethren, seek out from among you seven men of good reputation, full of the Holy Spirit and wisdom, whom we may appoint over this business; but we will give ourselves continually to prayer and to the ministry of the word."

And the saying pleased the whole multitude. And they chose Stephen, a man full of faith and the Holy Spirit, and Philip, Prochorus, Nicanor, Timon, Parmenas, and Nicolas, a proselyte from Antioch, whom they set before the apostles; and when they had prayed, they laid hands on them. Then the word of God spread, and the number of the disciples multiplied greatly in Jerusalem, and a great many of the priests were obedient to the faith. And Stephen, full of faith and power, did great wonders and signs among the people (*Acts 6:1–8*).

Obviously a team approach enabled the Jerusalem church to be much more effective than it otherwise would have been. May we have this similar outcome in our churches today: "the word of God spread, and the number of the disciples multiplied greatly."

3. Increased Productivity

More can be accomplished together than separately: "Two are better than one, because they have a good reward for their labor" (Ecclesiastes 4:9). Two great Old Testament characters, Moses and Aaron, exemplify this principle. As you know, Moses was gifted in leadership but wasn't a communicator. What Moses lacked in communication, however, Aaron excelled in. As a team, they led God's people on a march to the Promised Land. Two were better than one!

It's the same in the church. Dedicated leadership should delegate tasks based on individual gifts with determination to fulfill a common goal. There are six specific ways that ministry effectiveness is increased by the development of Ministry Action Teams:

- They expand the power of information and ideas through networks of sharing.
- They establish community, thus meeting people's psychological and spiritual need to be with others.
- They enlarge ministry opportunities through specialization by focusing on spiritual gifts.
- They make it possible for improved learning and decision-making to take place.
- They create synergy, which builds on the expanded possibilities and potentials of interfacing spiritual gifts and ministries.
- They help the church overcome the latent or residual effect of individual biases.

Not Just New Programs and Committees

Changing to a team-building ministry should be approached not as if it were an afternoon jog. It is not just another exercise routine or program added to the existing list of things to do. Before attempting this change, we should first build focus, commitment, and spiritual grounding.

The central issue in the move to a team ministry is to decentralize leadership. Although traditional committees involve people doing ministry together, they have often been formed by simply recruiting from some other committee, and they often lack effectiveness.

A Focus on the Family survey of pastors in thirty-six different denominations revealed that unrealistic expectations from church committees were a major source of frustration. Could it be that most of the burnout and restlessness among pastors comes from spending long hours with committees that show only marginal progress? Again, Roberta Hestenes says, "We must ruthlessly control the number and quality of the meetings in our lives if we are to avoid the 'numb pastor syndrome.' If our meetings can be transformed into the effective work of teams, we will see God renew, build, and use our people in a more helpful and effective way."

A special committee of dignitaries was appointed to meet missionary statesman Albert L. Schweitzer on his visit to America in the 1950s. Upon his arrival, the distinguished committee members lining the platform of the train station noticed that the doctor seemed to be looking past them toward the crowd. Much to the dismay of the welcoming committee, someone else had caught his eye.

With a cursory handshake, Schweitzer excused himself and went to an elderly woman in the crowd who was struggling with a large suitcase. Picking up the woman's luggage, he led her through the crowd, past the welcoming committee, to the steps of the train's passenger car. Dr. Schweitzer helped her up the steps, into the train car, and put her heavy suitcase in the overhead rack. Afterward, he went back to the distinguished committee and apologized for their wait. The welcoming committee had a *concern*, but Dr. Schweitzer had a *cause.*

Unfortunately, many church committees have a concern rather than a true biblical cause. Very little time is given to advancing the Kingdom by vision-casting, strategic planning, or evangelism and discipleship. In fact, as a church gets larger, it becomes increasingly more difficult to become proactive in these vital areas of ministry. Why? The pastor and other paid staff often get caught up in merely facilitating traditional programs.

Furthermore, churches under the committee system usually grow only to the energy level of the senior pastor. When the pastor runs out of steam, the church loses any momentum that has been built up, and this often results in discouragement and low morale in the church. Ministry Action Teams, however, are much more effective.

In his book *Team Building: An Exercise in Leadership* Robert B. Maddux makes a distinction between groups and teams. While teams are characterized by members who recognize their interdependence and common goals, groups are often merely a number of people working independently, though side by side. While members of a team feel a sense of ownership, members of a group see themselves more as "hired hands," since they are not involved in planning the group's objectives.

Maddux further cites a study of twenty coal mines. The study illustrates the increased productivity that results from going beyond the group paradigm to actual teamwork. The coal mines were in the same geologic structure, drew from the same labor pool, and were subject to the same governmental regulations. Productivity was measured in tons of coal produced per employee per shift. The mine with the highest productivity delivered two hundred forty-two tons per employee, contrasted with the lowest, which mined fifty-eight tons per employee.

The study concluded that the primary difference in the mines was the way in which company management worked with the employees. The most productive mines provided employees with significantly more individual responsibility and involvement in setting goals and solving problems.

While the establishment of ministry teams may be difficult, the final joys far outweigh the growing pains. Here are some of the benefits of forming strong ministry teams:

▶ Increased lay involvement

▶ A willingness to do things differently

▶ Team ownership instead of individual ownership

▶ An exciting climate in which to minister

▶ Unity and enthusiasm

▶ Clear ministry focus

▶ Encouragement as the norm

The natural world gives several examples of shared leadership. Engineers have used wind tunnels to calibrate why flocks of geese always fly in the V formation. They have discovered that each goose when flapping its wings creates lift for the bird flying next to it in formation. The entire flock gains more than seventy-percent greater flying range than one goose flying alone. From time to time, the lead goose falls back from the point position, and another assumes the lead without breaking the formation. Every goose takes the lead during a long migratory flight. Each contributes his or her unique talents to the overall effectiveness of the flock. It should also be noted that the geese who are following honk to encourage the one leading.

Ephesians 4 and the Corporate World

A crisis is occurring in most local churches today. Pastoral staff and laypersons put in long hours but see few lasting results. In Ephesians 4:11–13 the apostle Paul describes the primary function of leaders. According to verse 12, they equip the saints for the work of ministry, for the edifying of the body of Christ, until we all come to the unity of the faith and of the knowledge of the Son of God, to a perfect man, to the measure of the stature of the fullness of Christ.

Pastors of growing churches have already discovered that the job of pastoral ministry is simply too big for one person to handle alone. As Ronald E. Merrill and Henry D. Sedgwick have pointed out, "[Churches] beyond a certain size [about one hundred fifty] cannot be managed by a single person; a management team is required."[1] Although most pastors haven't been taught much about ministry teams in Bible college and seminary, learning how to form successful teams is crucial to the long-term health of a growing church.

> NO MATTER HOW MUCH WORK YOU CAN DO, NO MATTER HOW ENGAGING YOUR PERSONALITY MAY BE, YOU WILL NOT ADVANCE FAR IN BUSINESS IF YOU CANNOT WORK THROUGH OTHERS.
> —JOHN CRAIG

The corporate world models some of the best ways for those teams to function. Many corporate leaders have already discovered the usefulness of teamwork, not realizing that it is a principle established in the pages of the Bible thousands of years ago. However, church leaders must be quick to recognize the critical difference between corporate marketplace teams and ministry teams in the local church. According to R. Daniel Reeves,

The core beliefs of church leaders form the foundation for team ministry: Our convictions about humility and brokenness come from God, not popular psychology. Prayer and the study of God's Word, not management theory books, create the passion for team ministry and prompt our desires to yield to God's will. It is God who is the instigator and sustainer of healthy, functional team relationships.[2]

TEAM STYLES

While the Bible must always be our foundation for the team model, the corporate world can teach us some practical lessons on how leadership teams function. Notice three different team styles from the corporate business world.

Employee Teams

In businesses that have employee teams, there still is a key decision-maker that sets the policies and goals. This person has ultimate control, and the team literally works for him or her. Two important questions are raised in trying to use such a model in a church setting: (1) Do you as the senior pastor really want that much control? and (2) Is this the kind of leadership and discipleship philosophy you want to foster? The corporate world and the church share one thing: The key to effective employee teams is giving each team member a sense of significance.

Small Partnerships

In the corporate model of small partnerships, the leader exchanges some of his or her control for shared ownership. The leader is then able to enjoy the assistance of team members who have a real stake in the success of the organization. In comparison with the members of an employee team, colleagues in this type of organization are generally more highly motivated.

Big Ventures

In major corporations, teams with lots of talented individuals have the potential to accomplish great things—if the individuals can function well as a team. High-powered management teams in the corporate world require a self-confident leader and a sense of shared equity among the team members.

Stopping Failure Before It Starts

Most new businesses fail within their first five years. The reason they fail is often a result of the owner's inability to lead and manage. These business people fail to manage the resources available to them. They fail to manage their time and money, and most important, they fail to lead and manage the people they had gathered to help them carry out their dreams and goals.

On the other side of the spectrum, most successful businesses never fulfill the dreams their owner and founders envisioned. Again, the lack of ability to lead and manage puts uncontrolled limitations on these business people. The size of every business is regulated by the leadership capacity of its owner.

As ministry leaders, we may be tempted to ignore principles that come from secular business management. However, many of these principles are biblical and are just as valid in the church as they are in any business. Most would agree that the size of any church is also regulated by the leadership capacity of its pastor. Leadership is not something that starts at the low end of the spectrum and grows steadily until it reaches its maximum. Leadership is developed on plateaus. For businesspeople (or pastors) to expand their capacity in leadership, they must grow within these plateaus.

PLATEAUS OF LEADERSHIP

Plateau 1: The Owner/Operator

The first plateau of leadership in business is the *owner/operator*. This individual goes into business for himself or herself and does everything that needs to be done. He or she owns it and operates it—makes the product, performs all the office functions, sweeps the floors, scrubs the toilets, does whatever needs to be done. The owner/operator is usually an entrepreneur—a person who is willing to go out on a limb and take all the risks.

In the church the first plateau may be called the church planter. The church planter starts a church or simply takes over a smaller church and does basically the same thing as the owner/operator in business. This person takes care of the "business" of the church: prepares and preaches the sermons, serves as the Sunday School superintendent, and teaches Sunday School. Basically, just like the business owner/operator, the church planter does everything that has to be done in the church. And at this stage of the game, this might be okay. The church planter may be the only one qualified to do the job, and the job must be done. However, this singlehanded role should not continue forever.

Plateau 2: The Proprietor

The second plateau, the *proprietor,* has the same effect for the businessperson as for the pastor-leader. They both realize they can no longer do it all themselves. How do they know? It's simple: their spouses are threatening to leave them! Their time is consumed with their business or their church. They no longer have time for family or any other activities. They find that they cannot work twenty-eight hours per day, and they soon come to the conclusion that if their business (or ministry) is going to prosper, they will need a team. They must delegate some of these tasks to others.

However, instead of fully stepping up to Plateau 2 and becoming managers, many business people mistakenly fall into what is called the *founder's trap* and become proprietors. (The term *proprietor* is typically associated with smaller businesses.) Proprietors decide to hire people to help them. The proprietor falls into the founder's trap because he or she has not learned how to build a team. When the proprietor hires helpers, that is all they are—helpers. The boss still drives the truck; the helper goes along to hand the tools. The boss still does the paperwork; the helper "assists" with clerical functions. What the proprietor fails to do is to utilize the strengths of the helper. The helper is given only some distasteful duties such as cleaning the toilet, stocking the shelves, or simply "helping" with the tasks.

If the businessperson does not learn to develop a team and remains instead in the same relationship with the one, two, or three helpers, the business's growth is hindered, because growth still directly revolves around the function of the owner. In essence, the owner has become the limiting factor to the size of the business.

In church ministry, pastors also fall into the founder's trap and become what we call Ephesians 4 servants. Instead of becoming leaders of their people, their role is limited to being servants to their people. Again, everything revolves around the pastors, and they become the limiting factor to the size of their church.

For the businessperson who does not get caught in the founder's trap, the next step or plateau should be to become a manager. Managers hire a team to work for them. They equip and lead their team to carry out the purpose of the organization.

In the church the next plateau for the pastor is to become an Ephesians 4 pastor, who leads, feeds, and equips the people. In Ephesian 4:11–12 certain gifts are mentioned, including pastor-teacher: "And He Himself gave some to be apostles, some prophets, some evangelists, and some pastors and teachers, for the equipping of the saints for the work of ministry, for the edifying of the body of Christ." The pastor was given for the equipping of the saints for the work of the ministry. That means the pastor is coaching the saints—building team members for the work of the ministry—so that the Body of Christ may be edified. In other words, the pastor (coach) equips the team so the members can do the work of the ministry.

Instead of hiring staff like the business person, the Ephesians 4 pastor takes advantage of the workforce already available—the laypeople—a team of Christians already gifted by God. The pastor (coach) trains them to utilize their gifts. This provides everything the workforce needs. When the pastor can no longer lead the team alone, then—and only then—should additional staff be hired.

Ephesians 4 pastors are stewards of the gifts, talents, and abilities of those entrusted to their care. A true Ephesians 4 pastor says, "I am not here to do the work of the ministry by myself. I am here to equip my people, build them up, train them, and educate them so they will be enabled for ministry." The job of Ephesians 4 pastors is twofold: (1) to develop the spiritual gifts of their team and (2) to provide areas of service where they can exercise those gifts.

As the church grows, more help will be needed. To avoid prematurely hiring staff, pastors should first draw help from their congregation. If they hire more staff before that, they're sending their church in the wrong direction and will train their staff to do the same thing they are doing—the work of the ministry rather than involving the laypeople. At best, they're building a spectator church.

Even when the pastor learns to train laypersons for ministry, the time may come when the Ephesians 4 pastor cannot train and keep all the laypeople involved on his or her own. Such a pastor must eventually become a multi-staff pastor, working with the laypeople and training them to minister first. Then when paid staff are added, they will all be going in the same direction. The added staff will continue what the pastor started—training and leading the laity to do the work of the ministry.

Plateau 3: The Executive

In business, the next plateau is the *executive* stage. Basically, the executive's job, like the manager's, is to manage people. The executive studies, analyzes, gives direction, and motivates, managing the team by managing the managers. The managers in turn manage the workforce.

On the church side, Plateau 3 involves the multi-staff pastor who delegates responsibility to the staff team. The staff oversees the church team—the laity. When the pastor says, "Staff, here is what we need to do," he or she wants them to see that it gets done. Pastors should delegate through the laity before they delegate to a staff person, and they should train their staff to do the same. In that way, laypersons become an extension of the pastoral staff ministry.

GETTING TO THE NEXT PLATEAU

Pastors must grow through one plateau to get to the next. They cannot successfully go from the church-planter stage straight to the multiple-staff stage. Coaching is the only way to become a true Ephesians 4 pastor. Pastors coach in a team ministry, members learning what their gifts are and understanding where they fit into the ministry of the church. Pastor-coaches also understand that exercising their gifts is part of a team effort with the rest of the Body of Christ, enabling a dynamic release of ministry both within the church and outward to a lost world.

To some, building these teams can seem like an enormous and daunting task that works only for those pastors who are already successful. That need not be the case. Team building can occur—and should occur—with any pastor, regardless of the location or the size of the congregation. However, the first step in building a team is for the pastor to begin to think of himself or herself as a coach who directs a group of special teams, not a servant who tries to meet all the needs of the congregation. Even before the teams are created, the pastor must have a clear concept of what it means to function as a pastor-coach.

On *Leadership Today,* a denominational television series I hosted for several years, Dale Galloway pointed out that teams made up of the laity could easily perform the majority of functions currently occupying the schedule of most pastors.

Dale said, "Ten ministry activities often fill a parish pastor's day." See the list below, and check only those activities that laity could not share with the pastor.

- ▸ Pray for the congregation
- ▸ Care for the sick
- ▸ Disciple other believers
- ▸ Train ministry leaders
- ▸ Study and teach the Bible
- ▸ Tell others about Jesus
- ▸ Represent the church at community events
- ▸ Visit newcomers to the church
- ▸ Run errands for the church office
- ▸ Encourage people through hard times

If pastors truly shared ministry based on the Spirit-anointed gifts of lay ministry teams, I don't think we would find anything that they could not do in ministry! Church history teaches that whenever clergy become the elite ministry "doers," the congregations they serve stagnate and die.

To review a bit of Church history, by 300 A.D. the Church was growing so fast that conceivably the whole world could have been converted during the next two hundred years. But Roman emperor Constantine made a near-fatal error. He decreed that everyone in the Roman Empire was already a "Christian." People who didn't really know Christ couldn't introduce Christ to others.

An elite clergy and a pagan laity put the growth of Christianity on hold. Conversely, when lay believers in Christ joined with each other—and with the clergy—in meaningful team ministry, the Church thrived.

Perhaps you should hang this helpful acronym on your office wall as a reminder of the fruitfulness that comes with team ministry:

Together

Everyone

Achieves

More **M**inistry

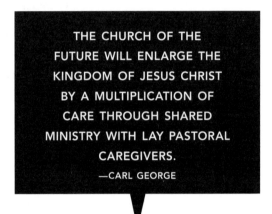

THE CHURCH OF THE FUTURE WILL ENLARGE THE KINGDOM OF JESUS CHRIST BY A MULTIPLICATION OF CARE THROUGH SHARED MINISTRY WITH LAY PASTORAL CAREGIVERS.

—CARL GEORGE

DEFINING THE TEAMWORK VISION

Team-building is not something that will happen automatically. The pastor must have a clear vision for it. Consider these four goals for team ministry in the local church:

- ▶ Organizing the team to discover and fulfill the Great Commission
- ▶ Empowering the team to reach the community for Christ
- ▶ Communicating ministry accomplishments to the congregation
- ▶ Relating to one another in a manner that pleases God

Ready or not, we are on the verge of a major change in the way we do church. This reformation is absolutely necessary if the church is to minister effectively in the present age. Melvin Steinbron, after observing the changes in the lay ministry's role over four decades, concludes, "In the first reformation, the church gave the Bible to the people. In the second reformation, the church gave the ministry to the people." Elton Trueblood, a pioneering writer about the need for lay ministry, wrote in even stronger terms: "If the average church would suddenly take seriously the notion that every lay member—man or woman—is really a minister of Christ, we could have something like a revolution in a very short time."

Generation	Reached for Christ
Builders (Born before 1946)	65%
Boomers (Born between 1946 and 1964)	35%
Busters (Born between 1964 and 1977)	15%
Bridgers (Born between 1977 and 1994)	4%

Eighty-one percent of Christians accepted Christ before they were twenty years old, and the youngest Bridgers are already older than that. This indicates that without some drastic changes, we stand very little chance of reaching much of the two younger generations for Christ.

The subject of change was addressed in The McIntosh Church Growth Network newsletter: "Minor changes are small modifications made without a corresponding shift in the perception of reality. Major changes occur when people develop a new perspective and act in new ways. . . . Transformational change comes only through radical modification in belief and practice."[3]

It's time for *transformational change*. It's time for a new way of thinking about church ministry. It's time to train a host of *coaches* (Ephesians 4 pastors) who will call their *players* (laypersons) from the comfort zone of the bench to the courage zone of the playing field and influence our world for Christ—while there is still time.

▷ Team-Building Tips

- ▸ Share team mission, vision, and values at an annual retreat gathering.
- ▸ Ask ministry teammates what you can do to help them do a better job.
- ▸ Give positive reinforcement for skills enhanced and developed.
- ▸ Update team members frequently on ministry progress.
- ▸ Instead of "great idea, but not for us," try "great idea—let's try it!"
- ▸ Remember the names and interests of your ministry team members.
- ▸ Give team members the resources they need to do the job.
- ▸ Provide a learning environment.
- ▸ Try reaching a consensus. A majority vote does not guarantee validity.
- ▸ Establish deadlines; then measure the team's ability to meet those deadlines.
- ▸ Let the team determine the deadlines.
- ▸ Cultivate a sense of ownership for the vision with the entire team.

▷ Resource Tip
Your Church's Personality

What is the *personality* of your congregation? Every church has a personality—a distinct way of thinking and doing things. That personality may be reflected in the church's official mission statement or may simply be part of the unofficial church culture. For guidance on creating a personality statement that fits your congregation, see Section 1 of *Church Operations Manual: A Step-by-Step Guide for Effective Church Management,* by Stan Toler.

2

DEVELOP YOURSELF AS A LEADER

GET OUT OF YOUR COUNTRY, FROM YOUR FAMILY AND FROM
YOUR FATHER'S HOUSE, TO A LAND THAT I WILL SHOW YOU.
I WILL MAKE YOU A GREAT NATION; I WILL BLESS YOU AND
MAKE YOUR NAME GREAT; AND YOU SHALL BE A BLESSING.
I WILL BLESS THOSE WHO BLESS YOU, AND I WILL CURSE
HIM WHO CURSES YOU; AND IN YOU ALL THE FAMILIES
OF THE EARTH SHALL BE BLESSED.

—GENESIS 12:1–3

▲

The great patriarch Abraham was a lot like Christopher Columbus on his journey to a new land. He didn't know where he was going when he started out, and he didn't know where he was when he got there. Abraham, by faith when called to a place he would later receive as his inheritance, obeyed and went, even though he did not know where he was going (Hebrews 11:8). Abraham may not have known *where* he was going, but he knew *why*. God had called him. God's plan was now Abraham's purpose.

As a team leader, you may often feel the same. You are headed toward a destination that isn't completely clear at the outset. You understand that change is necessary and that you must re-imagine the way you have been doing ministry. You feel a sense of God's call in this—you understand that you are undertaking a spiritual journey toward effective servanthood. Like

Abraham, you realize that you must set out first and fill in some of the blanks as you move along. You will have to develop a vision, a team, and a new way of leading others. And the main thing you will need to develop is yourself. You must become a leader who is capable of leading others in a new way. That will require development in three vital contexts: *spiritual leadership, personal leadership,* and *interpersonal leadership.* In this chapter you will explore some of the important qualities of a team leader.

> GIVE US CLEAR VISION THAT WE MAY KNOW WHERE TO STAND AND WHAT TO STAND FOR, BECAUSE UNLESS WE STAND FOR SOMETHING, WE SHALL FALL FOR ANYTHING.
>
> —PETER MARSHALL

SPIRITUAL LEADERSHIP: CONSECRATION

As a ministry leader, you have answered God's call upon your life. Though we are busier than ever, many of us live our lives rather aimlessly at times—even though our intentions are noble. At work we desire to be the consummate professional. At home we seek to be the ultimate spouse or parent. At church we are the devout believer. In spite of our involvement, it often seems that there's something missing in our lives: we lack power.

A consecrated life is a life devoted to a single purpose. It settles on God's plan, no matter the consequence. What may we expect from such a consecrated life? What is the result of consecrating our lives to Christ, making His will our main objective? In a word, *power.*

Focus

That power of consecration rises from an increased focus. When you understand the big picture, it's easier to put the little things in place. A consecrated life is focused on serving God. That makes every decision—from vocational choices to moral decisions—much easier to make. Consecration brings the power of focus.

Endurance

That power also produces great endurance. There is no more noble cause than Christ's—no more valid reason to persevere in spite of pain or persecution. When your life has been laid at the feet of the Master, when His cross is squared firmly across your shoulders, you will have the strength to face life even at its worst. Insults are easier to bear, sacrifices easier to make.

Victory

That power brings certain victory. That term may be as obsolete as an Edsel at times, but "victory" is still the believer's greatest incentive. Paul put the promise in writing: "Thanks be to God who always leads us in triumph in Christ, and through us the fragrance of His knowledge in every place" (2 Corinthians 2:14). The consecrated person is a victorious soldier for Christ—even before the battle begins. Whether the struggle is against temptation in our own lives or the struggle against the forces of spiritual darkness in the world, the believer with a single focus is able to endure. Consecration brings victory.

The Scriptures bear it out. The writer of Hebrews mentions other "hall of fame" Christians who had consecrated themselves to God, those who had placed their lives on the altar of devotion and let them burn, others who were hopelessly devoted to their God. What was the result in their lives? Just read.

> What more shall I say? I do not have time to tell about Gideon, Barak, Samson and Jephthah, about David and Sam-

uel and the prophets, who through faith conquered king-
doms, administered justice, and gained what was promised;
who shut the mouths of lions (*Hebrews 11:32-33*, NIV).
And there is one name missing from that list: yours. By faith
you, too, may become one of these of whom the world was not
worthy. By faith you, too, may be consumed by a passion for God
that burns away every thought, every motive that is not focused
on His will. By faith you may endure any hardship, achieve any
victory. By faith you may prevail. That's the power of a consecrated life, the prime requisite for spiritual leadership.

SPIRITUAL LEADERSHIP: HOLINESS

Do you remember the first time you heard your own voice re-
corded and played back? You probably reacted like many others:
"Do I really sound like that?" Or have you ever had a picture taken
and then, upon seeing it, remarked, "That doesn't look like me!"
Isaiah had a similar struggle with sight and sound.

In the year that King Uzziah died, I saw the Lord seated
on a throne, high and lifted up, and the train of his robe filled
the temple. Above it stood seraphim; each one had six wings:
with two he covered his face, with two he covered his feet,
and with two he flew. And one cried to another and said,
"Holy, holy, holy is the LORD of hosts; the whole earth is full of
his glory!" And the posts of the door were shaken by the voice
of him who cried out, and the house was filled with smoke.
So I said: "Woe is me, for I am undone! Because I am a man of
unclean lips, And I dwell in the midst of a people of unclean
lips; For my eyes have seen the King, The Lord of hosts" (*Isaiah 6:1-5*).

Isaiah saw the holiness of God and heard the reaction of the
adoring angels in its presence. He then looked at himself and
said, "That doesn't look like me. I don't sound like that."

I've seen some folks try it, but God's holiness is pretty hard to fake. They usually end up looking grim and joyless—as if they had been baptized in embalming fluid. What an inaccurate reflection of God's holiness! And how out of tune they are with the seraphs who sing around His throne!

I would rather be around the genuine. C. S. Lewis said in *Letters to an American Lady*, "How little people know who think that holiness is dull. When one meets the real thing, it is irresistible." Isaiah gave us a glimpse of the wholly genuine seated on a throne, high and exalted.

Looking so out of place in God's presence, the prophet expresses an agonizing longing to reflect what God truly is—holy. But what does holiness look like?

We have a problem here. We're like the Sunday School student who was asked to draw a Bible picture. "What's that?" her teacher asked after seeing the "masterpiece."

"That's God," the student quickly replied.

Concerned, her teacher commented, "Honey, none of us knows what God looks like." Puzzled, the student replied, "Well, if we don't know what He looks like, then how can we be like Him?"

I'm glad that God solved the problem by giving us a glimpse of himself in His Word—as much as we can stand this side of eternity. "Since the creation of the world His invisible attributes are clearly seen, being understood by the things that were made, even His eternal power and Godhead, so that they are without excuse" (Romans 1:20).

In the Old Testament He is seen in the awesome and unapproachable majesty of the throne, the burning bush, or the Ark of the Covenant. Later in the New Testament He is seen in the redemptive vulnerability of the manger cradle, the executioner's cross, or the borrowed grave. Holiness characterizes God. And that holiness must be reflected in His people. "It is written: 'Be holy, because I am holy'" (1 Peter 1:16).

It seems implausible at first. Reflecting God's holiness? Because of who He is, He could never be like us. But also because of who He is, He invites us to be like Him—as much as we can be while living in the confines and confusions of planet earth. The impossible becomes possible through the provision of His Son, Jesus Christ, and the power of His Holy Spirit. Wesley said the Holy Spirit is the "immediate cause of holiness."

How then should we reflect God's holiness?

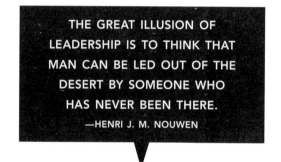

THE GREAT ILLUSION OF LEADERSHIP IS TO THINK THAT MAN CAN BE LED OUT OF THE DESERT BY SOMEONE WHO HAS NEVER BEEN THERE.
—HENRI J. M. NOUWEN

Flee from Sin

First, God's holiness is reflected in an unconditional hatred of sin. Proverbs 6:16–19 reads, "There are six things the LORD hates, seven that are detestable to him: haughty eyes, a lying tongue, hands that shed innocent blood, a heart that devises wicked schemes, feet that are quick to rush into evil, a false witness who pours out lies and a person who stirs up conflict in the community" (NIV). Reflecting God's holiness means rejecting sin. "No one who lives in him keeps on sinning. No one who continues to sin has either seen him or known him" (1 John 3:6, NIV).

Love Others

Second, God's holiness is reflected in an unconditional love for His people. "See what great love the Father has lavished on us, that we should be called children of God!" (1 John 3:1, NIV). God's heart looks beyond the deed to the doer. He can't accept the sin, but He can wrap His arms of acceptance and forgiveness around the repentant sinner.

As a boy attending camp meetings, I remember those times following a stirring service when we would gather for a time of praise and reflection around a campfire. One by one, as other young people arrived, the circle was enlarged. Some of those who joined the circle weren't necessarily the holiest in disposition or conduct (at least before the service). But the presence of God, the warmth of the fire, and the glow on our hearts made a place for them in the circle.

Reflecting God's holiness means no more closed circles. That doesn't mean stamping approval on sin—in any form. It does mean, however, having a heart that is inclusive rather than exclusive. In his message "The Way of Holiness" Jonathan Edwards declared, "[Holiness] is sweet and ravishingly lovely."

Giving to Others

Third, God's holiness is reflected in unconditional sacrifice for the welfare of others. John 3:16 has been mocked by football fans, wrestling promoters, and stand-up comedians. But it will never be replaced as the definitive word on God's commitment to His creation. "God so loved the world that He gave His one and only Son, that whoever believes in him shall not perish but have eternal life" (NIV). He loved, He gave, He paid the ultimate price for every person.

Reflecting God's holiness means the putting aside of self and selfishness for the redemption of others. According to Paul the apostle, that is seen in the home as well as on the highways.

Ephesians 5:25 admonishes, "Husbands, love your wives, just as Christ also loved the church and gave Himself for her." Chuck Colson said, "Holiness is the everyday business of every Christian."

Though we are not "little gods," as some religions teach, we can have a little of God in us. "It is because of him that you are in Christ Jesus, who has become for us wisdom from God—that is, our righteousness, holiness and redemption" (1 Corinthians 1:30).

A nineteenth-century Scottish theologian once wrote, "Holiness consists in thinking as God thinks, and willing as God wills." What is that? Reflecting the holiness of God! This is your role as a spiritual leader.

SPIRITUAL LEADERSHIP: PRAYER

Everyone depends on a leader for answers. Where do we go next? What's our goal? Should we move ahead or wait? It's the leader who must make these decisions, sometimes choosing between the greater of two goods—or the lesser of two evils. But where does the leader go for help? Effective leaders have learned this secret: they are not alone. When forced to make tough choices, they seek the counsel of one greater than themselves. They seek the guidance of God.

Pray for Perspective

Competence, skill, and intelligence are all important attributes of leadership. But there is one greater: faith. Truly great leaders believe in someone greater than themselves, and they express that belief in regular times of reflection and devotion. By spending time alone with God, leaders gain perspective. They are reminded of what really matters—and what doesn't.

Pray for Wisdom

Solomon, the wisest man in the Bible, was offered an incredible opportunity. God told him that he could ask for anything and receive it. Solomon asked for wisdom. As a result, he became the greatest king in the history of his nation. Great leaders pray not merely for specific needs, like better staff, more funding, or greater resources. They pray for something more fundamental, the wisdom to make proper choice. They pray that God will make them people of insight, discernment, and integrity.

Pray for Guidance

Even the most competent leaders ask for advice. Great leaders take their questions to God, asking for insight. They consult the Master Planner before announcing a new policy or strategy. They seek God's direction for specific decisions and for major goals.

Pray for Strength

When it comes to facing adversity, there are two types of leaders: those who go it alone and those who succeed. For great leaders, prayer is not a way out—it is a way through. The strength that is derived from communication with God sustains them through times of adversity. Prayer is a vital part of their spiritual support system.

Abraham Lincoln said, "I have been driven many times to my knees by the overwhelming conviction that I had nowhere else to go. My own wisdom, and that of all about me, seemed insufficient for the day." What was true for Lincoln must be true for all of us.

Remember that you are not alone as a leader. Make use of the most powerful weapon in the leader's arsenal: *prayer.*

PERSONAL LEADERSHIP: LIFELONG LEARNING

Maintaining a vibrant spiritual life is a primary focus of self-development for leaders. Personal life and growth are also important. If you are to develop yourself as a team leader, you will need to develop yourself as a person. One way to do that is to devote yourself to the habit of lifelong learning. Determine that you will continually grow and improve for as long as you live.

A farmer posted this sign on the pasture fence: "Trespassers welcome. Just be sure to cross the field in 9.9 seconds—the bull can make it in ten!"

In this fast-moving information age, it's easy to get left behind. Leaders stay ahead of those charging bulls by staying alert and keeping themselves informed.

Good leaders don't try to be experts in every area. They know what they know and what they don't. They understand the limitations of their wisdom and experience, and they fill in the gaps by asking questions, seeking counsel, and learning from others.

People who don't ask for counsel make unnecessary mistakes. Leaders are not bashful about asking for advice and not skittish about taking it. They cultivate counselors. They work on developing a network of associates who can plug modules of skill and experience into their lives. Here are a few of the places outstanding leaders look for advice.

> IT'S HARD WHEN YOU'RE UP TO YOUR ARMPITS IN ALLIGATORS TO REMEMBER YOU CAME HERE TO DRAIN THE SWAMP.
> —RONALD REAGAN

At Home

The best leaders are sensitive to the abilities and experience of their own associates. They seek input from the team and ask questions. They know there's no shame in being ignorant but that it's a crime to be negligent. They freely ask for information from those they know best.

In the Media

Leaders are readers. They learn how to pick the meat off an article or news item and leave the bones. They know what's in the news, and they keep up on trade journals. There is always a book on their nightstand, and they read blogs and news sites voraciously.

At Workshops

Continuing education opportunities abound in nearly every field, and the best leaders attend them, keeping current on their business or profession. They know that the price of registration for a good learning opportunity will be more than made up by increased sales, improved efficiency, or an influx of good ideas. They go to learn and take others with them.

At School

Education is an investment, and leaders put money in the bank of learning. They make the time to complete or continue their formal education. Online, on the weekend, or in traditional programs, they find a way to get that degree.

Are there gaps in your knowledge as a leader? In what areas could you use advice, information, or greater skill? What will you do to acquire it?

PERSONAL LEADERSHIP: PRIORITIES

Leaders make dozens of decisions every day. In fact, before you leave the house you've probably made several choices. Cereal or scrambled eggs, casual or business attire, do I have time for a second cup, or should I get going right now?

However, the most important choices you make are not about your personal choices—they're about importance. The things you decide to do will directly influence your energy flow throughout the day.

Here are four questions that will help you evaluate the importance of any opportunity.

Is it God-honoring?

Will your decided action maintain its integrity once it's strained through the filter of your faith? If it's not a Kingdom priority, it has the potential to drain your energy instead of enhancing it. My mentor and friend Elmer Towns once told me, "Greatness involves more than measurable achievement; it starts with the leader's heart and not his head. It is rooted in virtues like self-sacrifice, love, courage, loyalty, accountability, humility, meaning, mission, passion, and commitment. Those are Kingdom qualities, and your decisions must possess that dynamic."

Does it have an eternal dimension?

Does the proposed action merely result in accumulations on earth, or does it invest in eternity? Actions that are centered in the temporal are energy-0drainers. Will your proposed action increase your stock in the things of earth, or will it add to your account in heaven?

Will it add quality or merely quantity?

Those unclaimed jewels of Jesus' time, Mary and Martha, struggled with this very issue (Luke 10:38-42). Martha was too heavenly, and Martha was too earthly. Where's the balance? That's the important question. Once you reach adulthood, chores are usually a choice. But keep adding chores, and the result is fewer choices. Chores begin to dominate and soon siphon your energy reserves.

How will it affect my family?

The family is a God-given institution, but that doesn't mean were incarcerated in it. Interpersonal relationships with those we love the most should be joyous, not tumultuous. Adding an item to your to-do list might not be good for the family.

Every day you have a cash reserve of one thousand four hundred forty minutes. You can't afford to waste them on any activity that doesn't add value to your life and advance the goals of your organization. Because you *can* do something doesn't mean that you *should*. Evaluate every opportunity carefully.

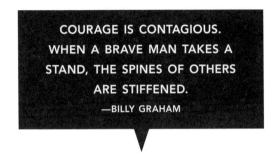

> **COURAGE IS CONTAGIOUS.**
> **WHEN A BRAVE MAN TAKES A**
> **STAND, THE SPINES OF OTHERS**
> **ARE STIFFENED.**
> —BILLY GRAHAM

PERSONAL LEADERSHIP: HUMILITY

A leader who is always looking for credit will soon be a solo performer. No team will follow a selfish leader for any appreciable length of time. The team may establish a good work regimen and perform well, but unless the members respect the leader, it will not excel.

The best leaders display that seldom-seen virtue called humility. They discover real worth in terms of their ability to generate team excellence, not personal recognition. Here's a snapshot of a great leader: a "big man" with a small ego.

Achievement Orientation

Great leaders don't care who gets the credit as long as the job gets done. Actions take precedence over accolades. Goals are more important than gold. Ribbons are incidental to right behavior. Great leaders don't draw attention to themselves; they express appreciation for the contributions of others.

Great leaders are willing to put the mission ahead of their personal agenda. They've discovered the greater joy of giving their lives for something worthwhile. The purpose, mission, and objectives of the organization are paramount, while the personality and personal achievement of the leader are secondary. Good leaders know that what they have done as individuals is far less important than what they can accomplish with and through others.

Thick Skin

Great leaders are quick to forgive. Small-minded people hold grudges; big people forgive and forget. Small-minded people nurse insults and look for revenge; humble people let bygones be bygones. All great leaders are big people. They earn respect but never demand it. They avoid petty squabbles and develop thick skins.

Others-Focused

Great leaders are gratified by the achievements of others. All good leaders realize that they alone can never accomplish all they dream about; others must help carry out their vision. So they invest, encourage, train, and enable them to succeed. The best leaders realize that there's plenty of success to go around, and they help those around them reach for the stars.

Great leaders give credit where it's due. They know that they are highly skilled, yet they realize that their success depends on the contribution of others. They know that there are no "unimportant people" in the organization; every person's contribution is significant. They're quick to encourage and lavish with praise. Good leaders know how to say, "Well done," and they say it often.

Enjoying great success does not depend on having a great ego. In fact, the opposite is almost always true. Those who think the most of themselves are usually respected little by others. Do you want to advance your goals? Learn to put others first.

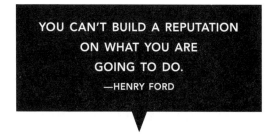

INTERPERSONAL LEADERSHIP: LISTENING

As you develop yourself spiritually and personally, you will recognize your need to develop in another vital leadership context: interpersonal relationships. We do not lead ourselves, and we do not lead things—we lead *people*! Therefore, your effectiveness as a leader will relate directly to your ability to relate well to others. If they trust and respect you, your leadership stock will rise. A primary way to gain that trust and respect is to develop the habit of being a good listener.

Here's a quick test of a leader's skill. Does the leader look into the eyes of the person speaking to him or her? If so, that leader is likely to be attentive, interested, and concerned about the needs of the team member. If not, the leader is probably distracted, unconcerned, or worse yet, egotistical. Good leaders take people seriously. They pay attention to words, inflection, and emotion expressed by others.

Listen to Ideas

Leaders listen to the ideas of their associates. They may not act on every suggestion, but they listen with an ear to hear fresh methodologies. Good leaders understand that the concept that will propel them upward may very well come from someone below them on the organizational chart. They welcome suggestions from teammates.

Listen to Complaints

Leaders also listen to complaints. Leaders understand that emotions left unvented can be become stifling at best, explosive at worst. Unresolved problems might very well suffocate the efforts of the team. Leaders value the feedback of both teammates and critics. They understand that the cries and concerns of others are cries for personal attention. And they listen.

Listen for Unspoken Meaning

Leaders listen for what is unspoken. They realize that a problem may be present for some time before a team member has the courage to voice it as a complaint. Leaders look for body language, expression, and other nonverbal clues to meaning. Like a well-trained mechanic evaluating the function of an engine, a leader hears the sounds that others miss.

Listen to Stakeholders

Leaders listen to stakeholders. Stakeholders are those whom the organization serves, whether they are called clients, parishioners, donors, or attendees. Good leaders listen to their constituents to find out whether their needs are being met. They pay careful attention to the feedback of those on the outside of the organization.

Listen for the Future

Leaders listen for the future. On a clear night you can hear a train coming from a long way. The sound is faint at first, almost imperceptible. But a careful listener can hear it. Leaders listen for the train that has not yet arrived. They look for trends that are just over the horizon; their ears are tuned for changes in the economy, the culture, and even politics. Leaders hear change coming long before it arrives. Learn to listen, and you will learn to lead.

> SOMETIMES I THINK MY MOST
> IMPORTANT JOB AS CEO IS
> TO LISTEN FOR BAD NEWS. IF
> YOU DON'T ACT ON IT, YOUR
> PEOPLE WILL EVENTUALLY STOP
> BRINGING BAD NEWS TO YOUR
> ATTENTION. AND THAT'S THE
> BEGINNING OF THE END.
> —BILL GATES

INTERPERSONAL LEADERSHIP: AFFIRMATION

Top performers, especially in the local church, are not motivated by a paycheck. They're motivated by an internal desire to achieve. Workers who are concerned with excellence have an inner source of inspiration. Good leaders recognize these excellence seekers and tap their hidden resources by praising their achievements.

Good leaders always know which team members are the standouts. Peak performers are usually the first in line and the last to leave. They are most often the last to complain and the first to cooperate. They are not inconvenienced by an assignment, because they have already sacrificed convenience for the greater good. These achievers work mostly for the pride of knowing that they have done the job well. Learn to praise them, and you will tap a reservoir of great strength.

Praise Often

Find ways to acknowledge those who go the extra mile for your organization. Often budget constraints prevent a leader from using money as a motivator. But there are other ways to recognize high achievers. Acknowledge their contribution at team meetings. Send an e-mail that says, "Thanks. You helped the team to-day." Look for ways to say thanks for a job well done.

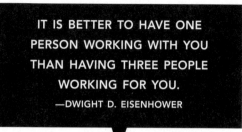

IT IS BETTER TO HAVE ONE PERSON WORKING WITH YOU THAN HAVING THREE PEOPLE WORKING FOR YOU.

—DWIGHT D. EISENHOWER

Increase Responsibility

When team members prove they're up to a challenge, give them one. Give an important assignment to your standout players, and they'll rise to the occasion. High achievers look for ways to increase their contribution. One way of saying thanks for what they've already done is to place even greater trust in them in the future.

Write It Up

If you have a formal evaluation process, use it to reward those who do well. Let their annual evaluations reveal the impact of their contribution on the organization. Give them an A for effort, and others will see their worth. If you benefit from the contribution of someone who is not on your team, send a positive note to his or her boss. Let that leader know that this team player is worth keeping.

Cut the Check

If you can use monetary rewards, do so to encourage your best performers. Even small bonuses or perks are meaningful. They say, "I value you!" loud and clear. Just be sure the reward system is fair and consistently used.

Thank you. They're simple words and easy to say. Use them often, and you'll keep your best performers working at high efficiency.

INTERPERSONAL LEADERSHIP: PARTNERSHIP

Why do some leaders succeed where others fail? Frankly, most of the time it's because successful leaders realize that success is a team effort. Leadership and partnership go hand in glove. One is fully dependent upon the other. Effective leaders value partnership, and they are always ready to join with someone who can contribute to a shared goal.

Counsel

"Two heads are better than one" is an axiom learned early in life. What, then, is the next level? Four heads? Eight? Sixteen? The pooling of wisdom and ability affords a greater opportunity for excellence. Efficiency generally increases with participation.

Communication

Leaders understand the importance of good communication. They know that a goal is nothing but a piece of paper until team members internalize it. Without the interaction of each member with another, the work will be disjointed and the team divided. Leaders work to foster communication between internal and external partners. They do not allow team members to work in isolation.

Cooperation

Marathon runners are rugged athletes. But they're not always leaders. Leadership depends on the ability to partner with others to achieve success. Great leaders are able to gather a collection of diverse people around a common purpose. They recognize that the whole is greater than the sum of its parts. They reach out to build bridges, create alliances, and foster cooperation. Leadership is a team sport.

Community

Leaders build morale and create community. They keep the mood positive. They compliment and praise individual and team efforts. They recognize outstanding achievements because they know that propelling one of the team members forward will push others to achieve more. Success is one part leader and nine parts partner.

Credit

When a good leader is credited for efficiency, he or she will always accept the accolades on behalf of others. Praising the team for its efforts simply motivates partners to greater efficiency. Great leaders create an atmosphere in which others can succeed. Then they share the celebration of victory with those who made it possible.

Stretch out your arm and extend your hand as far as you can. What is your reach—thirty inches? Maybe thirty-six? Now imagine joining hands with another individual, then another and another. You have extended your reach by at least three times. That's the power of partnership.

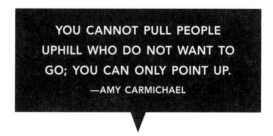

YOU CANNOT PULL PEOPLE
UPHILL WHO DO NOT WANT TO
GO; YOU CAN ONLY POINT UP.
—AMY CARMICHAEL

LEAVING A LASTING LEGACY

A television sitcom promotion included an interesting statement by the main character: "I learned about integrity from my father. He had five wives but never missed an alimony payment."

If worldly integrity is learned by the example of careless character, we are called to a higher standard. The integrity of a Christian leader speaks louder than a sharp PowerPoint presentation, a handful of brochures, or a stack of business cards. Integrity is something that can't be handed to you as you walk across the graduation platform. Integrity comes from within. It's the result of a focused faith, godly choices, right associations, and a tenacious commitment to truth.

When integrity is present in the life of a leader, it is a beautiful thing. When integrity is missing, life gets messy! Integrity may be one of the least-recognized qualities for new-millennium leadership, yet it will leave the greatest legacy.

Later on, when historians think about many present-day leaders, they will struggle to remember how many people reported to a particular leader and how many letters followed his or her name. What history will remember is how the leader conducted himself or herself. The leader will be known in the future primarily by his or her level of integrity.

In a publication called *The Cross and the Flag*, the power of integrity's legacy was chronicled in the lives of two men. One was Max Jukes, who lived in New York state. He was an unbeliever. Jukes had one thousand twenty-nine known descendants, of whom three hundred died prematurely. Of those who survived, one hundred were sent to prison for an average of thirteen years each; one hundred ninety were prostitutes; one hundred were alcoholics. Over the years the Jukes family cost the state $1.2 million and made virtually no contribution to society.

The second man, Jonathan Edwards, lived in New England at about the same time as Max Jukes. He believed in God and became a prominent Christian minister. Edwards had seven hundred twenty-nine known descendants. Three hundred became preachers; sixty-five were college professors; thirteen were college or university presidents; sixty became authors; three were elected to Congress; and one became vice president of the United States.

Integrity cannot be faked; the future will bring it to light. The most urgent question for any leader is not "What is my vision?" or "What are my skills?" The most vital issue for any leader to settle is this one: *What is my level of integrity?* The answer to that single question will shape your legacy for generations to come.

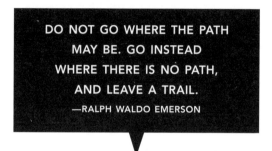

DO NOT GO WHERE THE PATH
MAY BE. GO INSTEAD
WHERE THERE IS NO PATH,
AND LEAVE A TRAIL.
—RALPH WALDO EMERSON

▷ **Team-building Tips**

- ▸ Devote every day to the Lord.
- ▸ Focus your energy on your top priorities each day.
- ▸ Praise your teammates often.
- ▸ Pray! Pray! Pray!
- ▸ Give away the credit for success; share the responsibility for failure.
- ▸ Manage priorities, not time.
- ▸ Read for thirty minutes each day.
- ▸ Spend time sharpening the saw.
- ▸ Immediately affirm good qualities in others.
- ▸ Keep your relationship with the Lord in good order.
- ▸ Communicate constantly.
- ▸ Develop partnerships inside and outside your local church.
- ▸ Flee from sin; pursue righteousness!

▷ **Resource Tip**
Your Personal Growth Plan

Many church leaders realize they must make a major shift in their thinking if they are to successfully integrate Ministry Action Teams into their local context. That kind of major change in thought may be accompanied by a need for intensive personal growth that may encompass other areas—including spiritual and personal life. Are you ready for a unique four-week growth plan that will help you gain clarity and control in your life and ministry? See *ReThink Your Life: A Unique Diet to Renew Your Mind,* by Stan Toler.

3

DEVELOP COACHING SKILLS

WHO THEN IS PAUL, AND WHO IS APOLLOS, BUT MINISTERS
THROUGH WHOM YOU BELIEVED, AS THE LORD GAVE TO EACH
ONE? I PLANTED, APOLLOS WATERED, BUT GOD GAVE THE
INCREASE. SO THEN NEITHER HE WHO PLANTS IS ANYTHING,
NOR HE WHO WATERS, BUT GOD WHO GIVES THE INCREASE.
NOW HE WHO PLANTS AND HE WHO WATERS ARE ONE AND
EACH ONE WILL RECEIVE HIS OWN REWARD ACCORDING TO
HIS OWN LABOR. FOR WE ARE GOD'S FELLOW WORKERS;
YOU ARE GOD'S FIELD, YOU ARE GOD'S BUILDING.

—1 CORINTHIANS 3:5–9

▲

While coaching football at the University of Colorado, Bill McCartney dared his 1991 team to play beyond their normal abilities. He had heard that most people spend eighty-six percent of their time thinking about themselves and only fourteen percent of their time thinking about others. The coach was convinced that if his team members could stop thinking about themselves and began to think of others, a whole new source of energy would be available to them.

McCartney challenged each player to call someone he loved and tell that person that he was dedicating the game to him or her. Each team member was to encourage the person he called to carefully watch every play, because the game was dedicated to that person. McCartney arranged to distribute sixty footballs, one for each player to send to the person he had chosen, with the final score written on the football.

Colorado was playing its archrival, the Nebraska Cornhuskers, on Nebraska's home turf. Colorado had not won a game there in twenty-three years, but Coach McCartney challenged his players to go beyond themselves—to play for love. The Colorado Buffaloes won the game, and the score written on sixty footballs was "27 to 12."

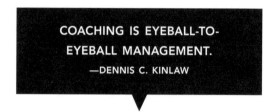

COACHING IS EYEBALL-TO-
EYEBALL MANAGEMENT.
—DENNIS C. KINLAW

WHAT MAKES A GREAT COACH?

Why do some teams attain levels of achievement far beyond the individual talents of the team members? It always involves a great coach and committed team members. As Darrell Royal once said, "The coach is the team, and the team is the coach. You reflect each other."

Successful coaches aren't always recognized for their achievements. In fact, the most effective coaches may seem to be invisible at times. As Lao-Tsu once said, "When the best leader's work is done, the people say, 'We did it ourselves.'"

According to my lifelong friend John C. Maxwell, "Success as a spiritual coach is directly dependent on your ability to influence your leaders." In this context, Maxwell has designed the 3-M Coaching Model, which stresses that an effective leader fills three roles:

1. Model

Most of us learn about eighty percent of what we know from what we observe. So the best way to convey the qualities needed for successful teamwork is to demonstrate them. If you want team members to be dedicated, then you must show them your commitment. If they are expected to put the team first, then the coach makes sacrifices too. If you want them to care for each other, then you must demonstrate your love for them. There's no substitute for showing them what you expect. Again, the apostle Paul wrote to his team, "You yourselves know how you ought to follow us, for we were not disorderly among you; nor did we eat anyone's bread free of charge, but worked with labor and toil night and day, that we might not be a burden to any of you, not because we do not have authority, but to make ourselves an example of how you should follow us" (2 Thessalonians 3:7–9).

2. Mentor

Good coaches also mentor their teams. They add value to their people by helping them grow, by encouraging them to be their very best. Like the New Testament's Barnabas, they are quick to give a good word of affirmation. Coaches who mentor team members see them not as they are but as they could be—building on the strengths of their team, teaching them how to shore up their weaknesses. Mentors are much more than advisers. While advisers may stand passively by and give opinions, mentors come alongside their people and walk with them during the most difficult parts of their journey. Great pastor-coaches not only watch from the sidelines but are also actively involved in the game.

3. Motivate

Coaches who want their teams to succeed must motivate the players. Parkes Robinson says, "Motivation is when your dreams put on work clothes." For a group of people to come together as a team and to accomplish the goal, they need to move from "great potential" to "great performance." They need to "put on their work clothes," and that requires motivation. Coaches must inspire their players with vision, praise their contributions, and give them incentives. People need to be shown how their vision lines up with the team's vision. They need to understand that a win for the team is a win for them personally.

Most people respond to team leaders they trust. Successful ministry "coaching" is more than a matter of understanding the mechanics of leading people. It also requires an ability to relate to people. President Abraham Lincoln had a clear understanding of this principle when he said, "If you would win a man to your cause, first convince him that you are his sincere friend."

Also, ministry coaching is never complete without the element of training. Seldom will the members of our church teams come to us fully equipped and fully trained. We must give them the necessary tools and resources that will help them develop their God-given talents and abilities.

CHARACTERISTICS OF GREAT COACHES

Great coaches have several characteristics in common. Whether in sports, business, or ministry, the best coaches will display most, if not all, of these traits.

High Self-esteem

Great coaches have high self-esteem. Coaches must have confidence in their ability to lead the team. It seems that everyone struggles with the self-esteem issue. But those issues can be settled when we see ourselves as valuable because of Christ's love for us, not because of something we can or cannot do. Ministry coaches need to understand that God has a lofty opinion of them. The psalmist captured the essence of that in his Spirit-anointed words "You formed my inward parts; You covered me in my mother's womb. I will praise You, for I am fearfully and wonderfully made; Marvelous are Your works, And that my soul knows very well" (Psalm 139:13–14).

Goal Orientation

Great coaches are goal-driven. They have a game plan, and they teach their teams to focus on the plan instead of the problem. You've probably seen professional coaches pace the sidelines with a piece of paper in their hands, referring to it before and after every play. That piece of paper has the game plan on it. It tells the coach what must be done if the team play is to result in victory. God has given us the game plan: "This Book of the Law shall not depart from your mouth, but you shall meditate in it day and night, that you may observe to do according to all that is written in it. For then you will make your way prosperous, and then you will have good success" (Joshua 1:8). Successful ministry coaches focus on God and His plan for their lives.

Communication

Great coaches are great communicators. They may have great knowledge and experience in their sport, but to be effective they must know how to communicate that knowledge and experience to their team. Jesus Christ never had trouble communicating with His team. They knew exactly what their ministry objectives were—beginning at Jerusalem, then on to the uttermost parts of the earth. Ministry coaches are well advised to study His communication skills. And those same coaches can turn to Him as a source of wisdom in communicating their hearts to their congregations.

Flexibility

Great coaches are flexible. They have to learn how to make on-the-spot changes. Circumstances arise—such as an injury to a vital member of the team—that require coaches to put their confidence in another player to finish the game. And sometimes even the game plans must be revised. Some circumstances call for Plan B. Successful coaches know when it's time to call a new set of plays.

Ministry coaches must learn to do the same thing. The we've-always-done-it-this-way approach to ministry often leads to being thrown for a loss. There are times when a new play—and even a new player—may result in a significant gain. Pastor-coaches should be flexible enough to accept each believer as a significant member of God's team and to appreciate the uniqueness that He has given each one.

Relational Skill

Great coaches are relational. To be effective, coaches must relate well to their players. Some of the greatest coaches of our time have been their players' greatest friends. Ephesians 4 not only tells the ministry coach how to communicate ministry skills to the congregation but also tells him or her how to build relationships with the members of the congregation. "Be kind to one another, tenderhearted, forgiving one another" (verse 32). The pastor-coaches who incorporate these relational guidelines into their ministry find the congregation eager to respond in like manner.

Supportive Attitude

Great coaches are supportive. They learn how to capitalize on their players' strengths and how to show compassion toward their weaknesses. Coaches must know how to work with both the strength and the weakness of the team and support each team member accordingly.

The pastor-coach will always be supportive of his or her team, no matter their strengths or weaknesses. But first that leader must learn to allow God to support him or her as well. It's too easy to get so wrapped up in the game and "serve God" without remembering that we must first learn to lean on Him. Only when we are *learners* can we truly be *leaders*, empathizing with those who must lean on us.

Passion

Great coaches are passionate. They're not afraid to show emotion. Some of the most well-known coaches in sports have been those who have openly displayed their feeling—and some of those displays have been notorious.

Jesus Christ himself showed a wide range of passionate emotions—from love to anger and from sorrow to joy. Remember that the Christ who gathered little children to himself in fatherly love also drove the moneylenders from the Temple in righteous indignation. Our culture often conditions us to hide our passion, but leaders who express a passion for their mission with a Christlike sincerity and a Spirit-controlled temperament motivate congregations.

Motivation

Great coaches are motivated. They don't depend on their teams to motivate them. They're already motivated, and their teams become motivated as a result.

Pray that God will ignite the fires of motivation in your heart. Pray that God will give you a burden to awaken the sleeping through vibrant team ministries. When your congregation feels and sees that motivation, the Holy Spirit will use it to motivate them.

Patience

Great coaches are patient. Professional coaches have higher expectations of a seasoned pro than a starting rookie. They know that part of their job is to be patient with the beginners until they develop into seasoned players.

When starting any new venture, it's easy to get discouraged if our high expectations aren't immediately met. High expectations are great, but a good dose of God-given patience will season our expectations and give us a balance that will help us fight discouragement.

Forgiveness

Great coaches are forgiving. They don't focus on the mistakes of their players; they focus on the player's correct attitudes and actions. Good coaches learn to move on. Last week's bad game could be a forerunner of next week's good game! Every one of us needs to learn how to "move on."

Let God's forgiveness be a model for our forgiveness when dealing with church members who don't see our new vision and attempt to create dissension. Before you implement the coach paradigm in your ministry, it would be wise to adopt an attitude of forgiveness for those who will inevitably get under your skin. Do what Christ did on the Cross, and choose to "pre-forgive" any future troublemakers.

HIGH PERFORMANCE
EXPECTATIONS ARE
CONSISTENTLY THE BEST
PREDICTORS OF TEAM SUCCESS.
—CLAY CARR

FIVE COACHING MUSTS

In addition, remember these five musts for becoming an effective coach to your team players from Alabama's legendary football coach Bear Bryant:

1. Tell them what you expect of them. Ministry team members should know how they fit into the game plan, and they should also know what you expect them to do to carry out that plan.

2. Give them an opportunity to perform. Team members should be given a chance to be a part of the "big picture" and carry out the vision.

3. Let them know how they're getting along. Verbal and written feedback gives team members an opportunity to learn, improve, and increase their contribution.

4. Instruct and empower them when they need it. Never be afraid to mentor the team when they seem uncertain. Always release and empower them to do the work after the training session.

5. Reward them according to their contribution. Here is one example. At Trinity Church of the Nazarene in Oklahoma City a partner in ministry is honored each month with a logo watch and a Five-Star Church Excellence Award Certificate.

KEEPING THE TEAM ALIVE

When we hear of someone's death, we often assume that the cause of death was some unpreventable physical problem, such as a massive heart attack, stroke, or cancer. Actually, there are at least three additional reasons people die: (1) they run out of friends, (2) they run out of money, or (3) they run out of purpose. Similar causes of "death" may be seen in the local church ministry. Let's examine those causes and see how Ministry Action Teams can be a great way of restoring life.

Friends

As a pastor, I've often seen people in the local church give up on life when a spouse or dear friend passes away. They experience a mourning of the spirit that erodes their physical health—and often results in death.

I've also seen churches "get sick" and "die" when people "pass on" to another church because they didn't feel as if they were a vital part of the previous church. Church growth consultants tell us that people need to bond with others if they are to remain active in a local church. They say that a visitor must establish a first-name friendship with seven to eight people, or he or she will not remain in that church. Ministry Action Teams give people an opportunity to connect. The small-group nature of ministry teams gives them an opportunity for friendship and fellowship. Ministry teams are kept alive through formal training times and informal fellowship times.

Money

Some people have physical conditions, such as diabetes, that demand expensive medical treatment. The disease itself may not be fatal, but when health-care funds and adequate treatment are not available, it becomes a deadly circumstance.

Likewise, vital ministries in the church can be dealt fatal blows by both a lack of funds and inadequate care. Local churches must be trained in the importance of supporting new ministries with their prayers and encouragement as well as with their dollars. And church leaders must be challenged to "go the distance" in allocating funds for those ministries.

Ministry Action Teams shouldn't be put on "life support." If they are to be effective, they must be adequately supported. The pastor-coach must seek to keep the team alive by clearly teaching the congregation about their value to the church's outreach and by going to bat for them in allocating funds for their ministries.

Purpose

Comedian George Burns had a cute saying: "I can't die—I'm booked till I'm a hundred!" On the day he died, *USAToday* announced, "And with no more bookings, George Burns died."

We've all heard of people who gave up on life because they seemingly had no reason to live. One key to keeping ministry teams alive is to constantly remind them of their purpose. A clearly defined, updated, and published statement of purpose for ministry teams is a great aid in maintaining ministry-healthy teams.

Entire churches can die for those same reasons. If churches don't focus on their purpose, or if friendships aren't maintained and membership dwindles, it will automatically result in a lack of funds. They are deadly "diseases" that if not corrected will lead to the church's demise. However, a lack of members and a lack of funds can normally be corrected if a church will grasp a clear purpose for its existence. There is nothing sadder than a church—or an individual Christian—that has run out of purpose. Perhaps that's why the average life span of a church is just thirty years. The church simply loses its reason for existence: knowing Christ and winning others to Him.

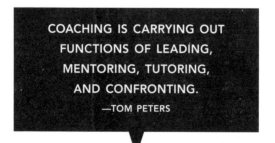

COACHING IS CARRYING OUT
FUNCTIONS OF LEADING,
MENTORING, TUTORING,
AND CONFRONTING.
—TOM PETERS

"Huddle Time"

One of the reasons sports teams huddle is to maintain their focus. In fact, a huddle serves a very important purpose for ministry teams as well. In addition to providing a time of focus, a huddle also gives the team an opportunity to listen, allows time and opportunity for personnel changes to be made, provides an opportunity for plays to be called, and allows the team to rest.

Another key element in keeping Ministry Action Teams alive is to make certain the team members have periodic huddle times.

QUALITIES OF EXCEPTIONAL PASTOR-COACHES

- ▸ They know Christ.
- ▸ They accept others.
- ▸ They are flexible.
- ▸ They enjoy challenges.
- ▸ They are self-aware.
- ▸ They value giftedness in others.
- ▸ They are courageous.
- ▸ They are supportive of others.
- ▸ They keep agreements.
- ▸ They share information freely.
- ▸ They are filled with the Holy Spirit.
- ▸ They listen.
- ▸ They facilitate others.
- ▸ They understand group dynamics.
- ▸ They understand process improvement.
- ▸ They know how to manage meetings.
- ▸ They know how to manage projects.
- ▸ They give feedback.
- ▸ They can let go of personal agendas.
- ▸ They resolve conflicts.
- ▸ They are good communicators.

A SENSE OF PARTNERSHIP MOTIVATES MINISTRY TEAM MEMBERS TO WORK EVEN HARDER.

—STAN TOLER

Part of being an exceptional coach is the ability to understand the dynamic of a team—what motivates them. Great coaches—and great pastor-coaches—are visionaries, because they see things differently than other people do. They are not bosses, commanders, or dictators. They know what "winning" looks like. They see their people as teammates—people with unique talents and a common purpose, not just a collection of individuals. They learn what makes the team tick. They learn how to motivate each individual. Exceptional pastor-coaches are continually developing their coaching skills.

Years ago in a small farming town, a grain mill was nestled beside a stream that flowed out of the hills. The most evident part of the mill was the wheel, which caught the water from the stream. Inside the building an axle ran from the wheel to the grinding stone that ground the grain delivered by the farmers. The source of power for the grindstone came from the water in the stream that flowed into the wheel's paddles and turned them, thereby turning the grindstone.

One morning the miller came to work after a bad storm. Several trees in the area had fallen and caused a lot of debris to be thrown around. When the miller checked his building before opening the mill, he found that there was only a trickle of water flowing down the stream. Limbs and other debris from the storm had dammed the stream, stopping the flow of water. There wasn't enough power to turn the huge wheel. Something had to be done.

The miller went inside and tried to turn the grinding stone himself. No matter how much strength he exerted, he couldn't turn it. Soon he realized that the day's work couldn't be completed unless he got power back to the paddle wheel. Finally he did the most obvious thing. He walked upstream and cleared away all the debris and limbs that had clogged the stream. Soon the wheel moved, and the farmers were loading the flour and meal as fast as he could turn it out.

Ministry wheels can come to a standstill too. Pastors can allow the "debris" of traditional ministry duties to clog their source of power. A study published in *Pastor's Family* revealed that the "pastor's average work week is 50 to 60 hours, and 80 percent of pastors feel that they are not adequately compensated financially."[1] If we're not careful, pastoral ministry can easily turn from delight to duty by continuing in the same traditional vein year after year, never really seeing any church growth or new converts and feeling comfortable in maintaining the status quo—when all the while God wants to clear away the accumulated debris and breathe His Holy Spirit into the church in a new and awesome way.

In order for this to happen, some changes must be made. We must allow God to remove the debris from our hearts, piece by piece, in order to get a new sense of His power and a renewed vision of what "working at full potential" means to Him. Like the miller, we need to get rid of the debris that clogs the power source and causes us to produce only a fraction of what God has envisioned for us.

ON BECOMING A PASTOR-COACH

Coaches are generally made, not born. In other words, few people are natural coaches. The great coaching skills we've discussed thus far must be learned. Making the change from a traditional pastor role to a pastor-coach will not be easy; the learning process will at times seem painful. Pastors tend to get set in their traditional ministry patterns and often find new methods difficult, especially when their church members are leery of change. Nonetheless, change must happen if we are to evangelize our communities. Let the following suggestions fuel the fires of change from being an ordinary pastor to an extraordinary pastor-coach.

Change Your Attitude First

Your attitude, habits, and focus all must change so that they are in line with the coaching paradigm. In terms of attitude, you must think like a *facilitator,* not a *doer.* With regard to habits, you must change from doing ministry by yourself to inviting others to partner in ministry. Also, with regard to focus, the key will be to focus on training the team.

The *New York Times* reported a change in the advertising campaign of a well-known cereal company. In their first television commercials, the actor portrayed a lethargic, low-key older man who was set in his ways. When sales began to decline, they knew they needed a new image—and some new commercials.

In the next series of commercials, the spokesperson, a veteran actor, underwent a complete makeover. Instead of portraying him in placid scenes of walking the dog or swinging on a porch swing, the advertiser shows him to be active and aggressive—riding horses, digging postholes, and building a corral. The spots were aimed at the growing older population and were intended to present them as a "take charge" generation. The increase in sales was dramatic.

The change in emphasis began in the mind of the actor. He had to convey an entirely different attitude to make the commercials work. A new presentation to a new generation demanded a new focus. It's the same in ministry. Pastors who want to effect change in their congregations and reach their communities in a new and exciting way must first of all experience change themselves.

Explain Your Changes to Others

Explain to your church why you've changed. Your new philosophy should not come as a surprise. For example, you could preach a Sunday night series of sermons that outline a scriptural basis for the new philosophy. The congregation must be taught that change is needed if your church is to steadily win souls.

Reaching a new generation demands some new methods. Things change, but the message must never change. There is still one Savior and one way to be saved. But the methods for teaching that message are subject to overhaul "to serve the present age," as Charles Wesley reminded us in song.

A word of caution: a teaspoon of sugar still makes the medicine go down. New methods must be mingled with old-fashioned affirmation, love, and a commitment to the welfare of your people. Force-feeding new ministries does not result in healthy churches.

Share the "Acts 6" model. In this well-known passage, the disciples were so consumed with temporal duties that they were forced to abandon the eternal.

> Now in those days, when the number of the disciples was multiplying, there arose a complaint against the Hebrews by the Hellenists, because their widows were neglected in the daily distribution. Then the twelve summoned the multitude of the disciples and said, "It is not desirable that we should leave the word of God and serve tables. Therefore, brethren, seek out from among you seven men of good reputation, full of the Holy Spirit and wisdom, whom we may appoint over this business; but we will give ourselves continually to prayer and to the ministry of the word." And the saying pleased the whole multitude. And they chose Stephen, a man full of faith and the Holy Spirit, and Philip, Prochorus, Nicanor, Timon, Parmenas, and Nicolas, a proselyte from Antioch, whom they set before the apostles; and when they had prayed, they laid hands on them. Then the word of God spread, and the number of the disciples multiplied greatly in Jerusalem, and a great many of the priests were obedient to the faith (*Acts 6:1–7*).

When the disciples could no longer focus on their ministry because of the mundane duties they were trying to do alone, they made a ministry change. And you'll notice they appointed team members!

When you share the Acts 6 study with your congregation, you may want to remind them of the McDonald's corporation motto: "We can accomplish more together than we can alone."

Define the Mission

This means determining and articulating questions such as *Who are we? What are we? Where are we going?* As author Stephen Covey says, "The statement of mission draws the organization together."

Paul Lee Tan in his *Encyclopedia of 15,000 Illustrations* tells of an experiment by the Minnesota Safety Council in which two drivers traveled the same one thousand seven–mile route in similar vehicles but at different speeds. The "fast" driver passed two thousand cars, braked one-thousand-three hundred thirty-nine times, and covered the distance in twenty hours and twelve minutes. The "slow" driver flowed with traffic, passed thirteen cars, and braked six hundred fifty-two times. It took the latter driver twenty hours and forty-three minutes—just thirty-one minutes longer than the fast driver. The fast driver used ten gallons more gas, and his pulse rate rose, probably because of the tension caused by the risks he had taken.

Without a clear mission, church leaders can be just like the "fast" driver. They expend a lot of effort, cover the same territory, but end up with a breathless—and tense—congregation. Conversely, church leaders who guide their parishioners with deliberate "travel plans" (mission) arrive at their destination with a sense of unified purpose and fulfillment.

Become a Vision-Caster

After much prayer, compile and communicate a yearly vision strategy for growth. Share your need of assistance from the congregation and the pastoral staff team.

J. Winston Pearce in his book *Planning Your Preaching* discusses the "chart that gives direction to your dreams."[2] His goal-setting advice includes the following:

1. Establish both short-range and long-range goals.
2. Set up tangible and intangible goals.
3. Learn to recognize obstacles, and then get rid of them by going around them or solving them.
4. Use initiative, imagination, and ingenuity.
5. Determine where you are now in relation to your goals, and measure your progress on a regular basis.
6. Set realistic and reasonable dates for reaching your goals.
7. Picture in your mind the rewards that will be yours when you reach your goals.

It's a chart that could be used in setting ministry goals as well. Vision-casting is integral to the health of the local church. Congregations are strengthened in knowing their leader has a clear direction for their future.

Involve Others in Ministry

It's very easy to fall into the Lone Ranger mind-set. Some pastors see the church as their own and think that if a job is to be done right, they must either do it themselves or closely supervise it. The truth is, a pastor's congregation existed long before he or she arrived and will most likely continue long after he or she leaves. No pastor can afford to start seeing himself or herself as the reason the congregation exists. The pastor-coach clearly sees that he or she is there because of the congregation and that the means to strengthen that congregation is through the active participation of its laity.

Continually Clarify the Journey

What parent hasn't spent the better part of a vacation trip answering the childhood query "Are we there yet?" The young passengers want to know if Dad or Mom has them on the right course. They're also saying, "How far have we come?" and "How much longer will it take us to get there?" That Q&A time is important to their sense of well-being.

It's the same when working with church ministry teams. They feel assured when they know that their leader has them on the right route. Team members must be given a clear communication of the "coach's" expectations and objectives. The very definition of the word *team* suggests clear goals and objectives to which all team members are committed.

Simplify, Simplify, Simplify

As Robert Kreitner often says, "Organizations should simplify so that an eight-year-old can understand how they operate." Legendary Green Bay Packer coach Vince Lombardi understood this success principle well. Once Lombardi was one of the speakers at a convention of coaches, and several of the other speakers had just described their elaborate offensive and defensive schemes. When Lombardi was asked his strategy, he replied, "I have only two strategies. My offensive strategy is simple: When we have the ball, we aim to knock the other team down! My defensive strategy is similar: When the other team has the ball, we aim to knock all of them down!"

Everything from training materials to ministry assignments should be given in the simplest terms.

CHANGES IN THE LIVES
OF DEVELOPING COACHES

As already stated, becoming a pastor-coach is a process that requires ongoing training, development, and change. Developing coaching skills will take some time and a few struggles. There are five lessons that are particularly crucial for pastors to learn in the early stages of their coaching development.

Lesson One: Realize That There Are No Perfect Pastors

I like the story of the pastor who went to a corner convenience store to buy a newspaper. He picked it up and took it to the counter, where he discovered that he had forgotten to bring any money with him—not even the fifty-seven cents needed for the newspaper. He explained to the clerk with embarrassment, "I'm afraid I don't have fifty-seven cents with me. I guess the only thing I can do is invite you to my church and preach a fifty-seven-cent sermon to you. But I'm afraid I don't have any fifty-seven-cent sermons!"

The clerk replied with a smile, "Don't worry about it, Preacher —I'll come twice!"

We won't meet the perfect pastor until we get to heaven. The bottom line is that we are human, and humans make mistakes. At times we will feel as if it would be better to forget the whole "change thing." But don't despair! Those feelings are simply a part of the growing process. Regardless of the mistakes we may make, there are still souls near our churches who don't know the Lord, and those souls need our ministry—imperfect as it may be at times. God uses people who are willing to risk new methods to reach them.

Lesson Two: Admit the Fact That a Pastor's Work Is Never Done

Some folks in the secular world complete their assignments. Cases are closed. Land is contracted. Games are won. Buildings are built. But a pastor's work is never done. There's always something more to do: more lost souls to win, more marriages to save, more sermons to preach, more lessons to teach, more administrative duties to oversee, more leaders to train.

Someone once said, "Great masterpieces are created by people who are out of breath." Our time on earth is short. We are following the One who said, "I must work the works of Him who sent Me while it is day; the night is coming when no one can work" (John 9:4).

Yes, there will be long days. And, of course, we will want to sit down by the well as Jesus did. But we picked up the cross knowing that the journey would be difficult at times. Our work on earth is never done.

Lesson Three: Focus on Your Gifts

Everything goes better when we operate in our areas of giftedness instead of merely reacting to every area of need. Elmer Towns teaches a principle he calls Division of Labor, based on 1 Corinthians 3:9—"We are laborers together with God" (KJV). His principle simply states, "God will not do what He has commanded you to do, and you cannot do what God has reserved as His authority."

Lesson Four: Concentrate on Your Calling, Not Your Critics

One study found that when a pastor is removed from a church, it is usually done by only a handful of disgruntled people. The loudest voice around you in your ministry may not be the voice of God. There's a lot of power in being able to smile and say, "I'm sorry you feel that way, but I love you, and God loves you," and go on with the task the Lord has assigned to you. You do not have to defend yourself against every criticism, and you undoubtedly will receive criticism. That only deflects energy from your calling and places your focus on the negative.

Remember: many of your critics see their own faults in you. Psychologists tell us that the things we don't like about others are the same things we have dormant in our own lives.

Lesson Five: Never Stop Learning

No matter how long you have been in ministry, it is vital that you maintain a teachable spirit and a willingness to change and grow. Henry Ford pointed this out in a perspective that we may apply to team ministry: "Coming together is a beginning, staying together is progress, and working together is success." Don't ever think you've arrived; keep learning and growing.

The apostle said it: "Not that I have already attained, or am already perfected; but I press on, that I may lay hold of that for which Christ Jesus has also laid hold of me" (Philippians 3:12).

Five Keys to Improved Coaching Skills

In his book *On Becoming a Leader*, Warren Bennis lists several important principles for those who want to develop their coaching skills.

1. Start with great people. You can't create greatness with mediocrity. Group leaders spend the appropriate time to find the right contributors to the group. They are often generalists instead of specialists.

A church should be built with people in mind instead of programs. There is nothing inherently wrong with programs; they are simply organized means by which to reach an objective. However, many churches make the mistake of building super organizations and super programs first and then later try to fit their people into them. Start with the people and their gifts (building the church by building them).

Someone has said, "Never use a great people to build a great church, but use a great church to build a great people." On the contrary, we should use a great people to build a great church,

DEVELOP COACHING SKILLS

and then use a great church to meet the needs of a great people. It is an unending and wonderful cycle: people ministering to people through the living organism called the church.

Even the secular world agrees with the philosophy of building people first. Today's leadership gurus emphasize this philosophy, saying that the key to making a person effective is to start with the person, find out what his or her strengths are, and put him or her in a position to make full use of his or her strengths. Never start with the job and make the person fit into the job or the program. Start with the person, and make the job or the program fit into his or her strengths. This will automatically minimize and render harmless his or her weaknesses. This is being people-centered in leadership.[3]

2. Create space for creativity. The more creativity, the greater the ministry. Every great group needs someone who can organize the genius of others. He or she must be a pragmatic dreamer and know how to create the environments for great projects to be successful.

Milton Bradley wanted to establish a career in the late nineteenth century creating board games. In just a short while, his games were found in countless living rooms in America. But his creativity wouldn't be stopped there. He had another idea. As a proponent of the kindergarten movement, Bradley saw the need for toys and teaching materials in the kindergartens.

Milton Bradley began to produce educational toys for kindergartens, though at that time kindergartens were quite rare. He had only a few customers to begin with, but within a generation there were more than three thousand kindergartens, and Bradley was manufacturing supplies for all of them—from crayons to child-size furniture.

Leaders must allow room for the Milton Bradleys of their church to set goals, adjust those goals, and set their sights on greater endeavors.

3. Inspire mission by operating from passion. The mission is always beyond them. It so focuses individuals beyond themselves that they make great sacrifices for the cause. People are recruited to crusades, not jobs.

Some folks are like the little girl who gave her version of the Lord's Prayer: "And lead us not into creation but deliver us from eagles." They are content to live in the land of "Status Quo," afraid to try new methods or soar to new heights. Leaders are just the opposite. They sing with the songwriter, "Still praying as I'm onward bound, 'Lord, plant my feet on higher ground.'"

What better cause is there to be passionate about than the church? It is the living, breathing body of a risen Christ. It offers hope to the hopeless, healing to the hurting, and forgiveness to the guilty through its head, the Messiah!

4. Galvanize response to both mission and "competition." Leaders focus on defeating the real enemy. They stand against Satan's intent to "tangle the church in the cobwebs of antiquity," as someone once said. They caution the team to move from "We used to do it this way" to "Let's try another way." Pastor-coaches will offer a challenge to the church to bring down the strongholds of the enemy (our real competitor) and build the kingdom of God in a refreshingly new, Spirit-led, positive, goal-oriented way. Paul Lee Tan wrote,

> After Mary Magdalene left the tomb (John 20:17–18), there is no evidence that any believer ever returned to it. Furthermore, there is no Gospel evidence that any of the enemies of Jesus ever visited the tomb. His enemies did not go, because they were afraid it was empty. Jesus' friends did not return to the tomb, because they knew it was empty!

5. Let vision enable mission fulfillment in concrete ways. Most church leaders are high on enthusiasm and low on planning. Churches need dreams with details and deadlines!

Bennis was right when he observed, "Deadlines create the urgency to get the work done. They force creativity, not perfection."

United States President John F. Kennedy was once asked how he became a war hero. With his customary dry wit, Kennedy responded, "It was quite easy. Somebody sunk my boat!"

Many church leaders operate from a "sunken boat" strategy. Instead of careful (and prayerful) calendar-planning, they create programs and utilize methods "just in time." Leaders could eliminate much administrative heartache that comes from last-minute plans and inadequate help by moving to a yearly calendar plan.

Add "Bench Strength" by Training Your Replacement

In his book *The Corporate Coach* James B. Miller writes of the necessity for leaders to train their replacements—a process he calls "adding bench strength." He tells of one manager who learned this lesson the hard way:

> Several years ago a warehouse manager came to me with sugarplums dancing in his head. It was time for his annual review, and he couldn't wait to tell me about all the things he had accomplished in the past year. He was already counting the raise he was sure he was going to receive.
>
> "I agree with you about your achievements. In fact, there are some additional things that you achieved that you don't have on your list," I said, after he finished making his case. "You've set the world afire this year. I have one question for you, however. Who have you trained to take your place?"
>
> "I don't have anyone."
>
> "Neither do I!"
>
> I then reminded him of the previous evaluations I had given him, how we both agreed that he would develop a successor so that he would be more promotable in the future as the company grew, and that there wouldn't be any additional pay increases until he had trained a replacement.

"Because you still don't have anyone in mind to take your place, I'm afraid we're going to have to hold off on any increase until you've trained a replacement."

He was shocked. But he began to take me seriously about the need to build bench strength. In fact, the next year, he had two people trained to replace him! All three of these individuals are still with us, and all have had promotions over the years because they developed replacements.[4]

Like the warehouse manager, many pastors initially resist the concept of training their replacements. After all, no one wants to be replaced. Successful pastor-coaches, however, must focus on adding "bench strength." An excellent coach so instills purpose and so trains the team that they can literally win without him or her. Likewise, a good pastor-coach should leave in his or her wake a legacy of fully trained laypersons who know how to function as a team in the Body of Christ.

A splendid example of a pastor who did this so well is Bob Russell. When Bob retired, he passed the Southeast Christian Church ministry torch to Dave Stone. With hundreds of trained leaders, Stone has continued the tremendous ministry growth pattern that Russell established in the Louisville, Kentucky, church.

On-site surveys at the Model Church Conference that I taught for twenty years have confirmed that the present pastoral philosophies in most churches include the following ten expectations. As you carefully read this list, check the items that could be considered a pastor-only task and the ones that could be performed by a layperson:

1. Pastoral care
2. Administration
3. Performing rituals
4. Leading meetings
5. Preaching
6. Teaching

7. Counseling
8. Vision-casting
9. Training staff
10. Recruitment

In addition to these ten expectations, some churches expect their pastors to mow the church lawn and serve as the church custodian. With the exception of Expectations 5 and 8, all the tasks named could be performed—and performed well—by laypersons, especially when they have been properly "coached."

To avoid confusion, pastor-coaches must clearly define the roles that are to be filled by their team members. Many Christians are aware of the tools (gifts) God has given them, but they don't know what they're to be used for: "Should I dig a hole with it—or saw a board? Use it to mix cement?" How can we expect laypersons to properly do the work of the ministry if they don't recognize what gifts they have and how they should use them? By showing them the purpose of the tools God has gifted them with and the way the tools work, we can strengthen the ministry of the team.

▷ Team-Building Tips

- ▸ Clarify your team ministry goals monthly.
- ▸ Conduct a brainstorming meeting every six months.
- ▸ Teach team members the value of constructive criticism.
- ▸ State the purpose of all team meetings.
- ▸ Have a team photo gallery.
- ▸ Clearly define job duties, responsibilities, and priorities.
- ▸ Start all team meetings on time.
- ▸ Visit team members on their turf in order to save time.
- ▸ Create a day for sharing innovative team contributions.
- ▸ Give credit where credit is due.
- ▸ Monitor team performance.
- ▸ Share ministry successes with celebrations.

How would you assess your current skills as a leader? Most pastors are aware that they need to grow in the area of leadership—especially coaching. Yet few have the resources for doing so. For additional help in developing personal leadership skills, see *Stan Toler's Practical Guide for Pastoral Ministry,* especially part 5, which deals specifically with coaching skills. Additional sections offer practical help in personal growth, family life, ministry, leadership, and communication.

4

ESTABLISH MINISTRY ACTION TEAMS IN THE LOCAL CHURCH

THE BODY IS NOT ONE MEMBER BUT MANY.
—1 CORINTHIANS 12:14

▲

"Down, Set, Wait!" Making Ministry Adjustments

Anyone who has watched a professional football game has seen this. The quarterback lines up behind the center, looks to the left and to the right at his linemen, begins the cadence, "Down, set . . ." Then suddenly he calls a time-out. What's wrong? The quarterback has taken a look at the defense of the opposing team and then looked at the formation of his own team's offense. Something isn't right. An adjustment needs to be made before play continues.

Behind that quarterback's decision is the experience and training of the coach. On any professional football team, the coach has spent years preparing for the task at hand and knows football inside out. Even though the coach isn't the one to snap the ball, the coach is the mastermind behind that action and the whole game. The coach is the one who has educated the team and taught them the methods by which they can win the game.

The same is true of the pastor-coach. Before he or she expects laypersons to become a collection of gifted ministry teams, solid education must take place.

For a church to grow, it must be healthy. A healthy church meets the needs of its members and reaches out to the community it serves. A healthy church is balanced, as Paul spells out in Ephesians 4:16—"From whom the whole body fitly joined together and compacted by that which every joint supplieth, according to the effectual working in the measure of every part, maketh increase of the body unto the edifying of itself in love" (KJV). A healthy church is increasing (growing in numbers by reaching people for Christ) and edifying itself (ministering to the needs within its own body). A healthy church ministers both to the body and those outside the body. A healthy church balances its ministry with the gifts God has given it.

People's Needs and God's Provisions

When my friend David Slamp was a young man, he had received no training as a teacher but was asked to teach a discipleship class. He soon realized that if he were to be successful he would have to tailor his teaching material to the needs of his students. Determined to become an effective communicator, he made an in-depth study of spiritual gifts. He discovered that there is a high degree of correlation between the needs of people and the spiritual gifts that God has provided to build up the church. The characteristics of each gift seem to meet exactly with a human need. The following chart lists the needs that the church must meet in a person's life if he or she is to mature as a Christian and show the spiritual gift that ministers to that particular need. Let's look at the needs one at a time and see how God has equipped the church to minister to them.

Team Ministry

Human Need	Team Member
Salvation	Evangelist
Awareness of Sin	Prophet
Doctrine	Teacher
Clear Direction	Exhorter
Guidance and Care	Pastor
Comfort	Giver of Mercy
Help	Servant
Financial Assistance	Generous Giver
Leadership	Administrator
Fellowship	The Entire Body of Christ
Maturity	The Whole Team

Salvation: Evangelism

First is the people's need for salvation. Romans 3:23 says, "All have sinned and fall short of the glory of God." Which team member meets this need in a person's life? It is the evangelist. This is not to say that the evangelist is the only person in a church to lead people to a saving knowledge of Jesus Christ. But if you took a poll, you would see that the evangelist is probably the one who has reached eighty or ninety percent of the converts. Evangelists are like salespeople for Christ. They are aggressive and confrontational.

Confrontational evangelists (sometime called *soul-winners*) try to motivate others to reach out to lost people. They tell stories that begin with "I went on a plane trip and happened to sit next to a guy who wasn't saved" and end with "As the plane touched down, the gentleman beside me bowed his head and accepted Christ as his Savior." They get onto an elevator with a non-Christian on the sixth floor and get off on the fourteenth floor with a born-again believer. Again, I need to stress that those with the gift of evangelism are not the only ones who can lead people to

Christ. But they lead more people to the point of decision, even though someone else may have influenced them and laid the groundwork for their decision to accept Christ.

Awareness of Sin: Prophet

Someone once said that the world is so churchy and the Church is so worldly that we can't tell the difference. The world has so much influence on us, even as Christians, that we sometimes have a hard time recognizing sin. The person who meets this need in our Christian life is the prophet.

Prophets tell the Word of God the way it is. They can see what's wrong in people's lives and point out what's wrong in a church, but their weakness is that they often don't have the ability to see what is right about people. Their ministry mostly manifests itself through preaching and usually that consists largely of pointing out sin. They do what we think of as hard preaching, often getting excited, "stepping on toes," and preaching for conviction. Their preaching will stir your heart and sometimes make you mad. These are typically what are called the "hellfire-and-brimstone"-type preachers.

Doctrine: Teacher

People need to know sound doctrine, or the principles for right living. Only the Word of God can truly tell us what is right. The person who meets this need is the teacher. *Didasko* is the Greek word that means *to teach*: to communicate knowledge, to relay facts, or to make known. Teachers are always studying and communicating the norms, standards, and doctrines of Scripture to others, verbally and through the written page.

Clear Direction: Exhorter

People need to know *what* to do and *how* to do it. The person who meets that need is the exhorter. Exhorters spend their time teaching people how to do things. They also motivate and excite people, enabling them to get more done. They make great counselors, because they tend to provide practical solutions to problems.

Care: Pastor

Everyone needs to be guided or cared for sometimes. Who meets that need? The pastor—sometimes called the *shepherd*. Shepherds have a caretaker approach to leadership. They are burdened to teach the Word of God and to care for the people around them. They protect and shelter their sheep. This gift is not limited to the position of senior pastor. Many Christians have the gift of shepherding, especially women. It can be used in a variety of positions inside and outside the church, from Sunday School teachers to den mothers.

Comfort: Giver of Mercy

People who are facing illness or other difficult circumstances need comfort. While there is no precise term such as *evangelist* or *leader* to describe this function, there are people who are especially gifted at showing mercy to others. These folks are usually soft-spoken but outgoing, seeming always to know what to say or what not to say when we hurt. They empathize with people, feeling their hurts and joys rather than just having sympathy for them.

If a tragedy were to happen in your life, you would appreciate a visit or call from the person with the gift of showing mercy, because he or she would help you deal with pain better. Mercy-givers provide a special support that others don't. They attract people who are hurting, because they have the ability to put themselves in other people's shoes. They also attract people who are experiencing times of joy. People like to share their happy days with them as well, because mercy-givers rejoice with them.

Help: Servant

When people need a helping hand, that need is met by a servant. Servants do just about anything—no job is too small or insignificant for them, no challenge too great. They thrive on meeting the needs of others in practical ways. Servants are content doing the physical labor around the church and many times at your house as well. Servants get fulfillment out of doing what many people see as menial tasks and are content working behind the scenes. They don't need or like the spotlight on them. They are not kings but king-makers. It's a gift that God has given to many believers.

Financial Assistance: Generous Giver

Finances are needed to support the ministries and the missions in the church as we meet people's physical needs. The person who meets this need is a giver. Givers are very mission-minded. It's not unusual to see a church with several givers in it, supporting many mission projects. While all Christians have the responsibility to tithe, God has given some the ability to give far beyond their tithe.

Many people with the gift of giving have the ability to make money, but not always. They usually like to keep their giving private and don't seek recognition. They are blessed by helping others in need and supporting special projects and ministries of the church. They are good stewards and want to know that their money is being put to good use.

Giving and serving are two gifts on which the church really needs to place extra emphasis today, because we've allowed the government to take over in these areas. We give to churches to add a wing on the church building, but when it comes to giving to an individual Christian, we rarely do that anymore. We've allowed the government to make up for our failure as believers to do what is right.

When a person in the church has financial problems, Christians usually say something like "Can you borrow the money someplace to get this straightened out?" or "Surely there's some type of welfare program that will help" or "You can have the money if you sign a note and pay it back monthly—with interest." We're telling people to go somewhere else, when God says in Romans 12:13 that the church in team ministry should meet those needs in people's lives, distributing to the needs of the saints and being given to hospitality. (See also Acts 6.)

Leadership: Administrator

Most people are followers. In order to reach a goal, eighty-four percent of the people need a totally planned, supervised program. If the program is carefully laid out, fourteen percent of the people are able to meet that goal with little supervision. However, only two percent of the people can create a dream and carry it through to completion by themselves. These latter people are administrators. They are the leaders.

Fellowship: The Entire Body of Christ

Everyone needs loving connections with other people. We all need fellowship. This need is met not by one subset of people within the Church but by the entire Body of Christ. This includes all the administrators, servers, givers, exhorters, prophets, teachers, evangelists, mercy-givers, and pastors. All these gifted Christians combined, the entire Church, must meet the people's need for fellowship. Polls have shown that most people who start attending a certain church do so for the fellowship they enjoy. We go to church to be with our friends.

Maturity: The Whole Team

If we look at the left side of the chart as if it were a math problem, what would we get by adding it all up? A mature Christian. After you have met all these needs in people's lives, they become mature. For every need we fail to meet, the people will be that much less mature. But the closer we come to meeting all the needs, the more mature the individuals will become.

Tragically, though, many churches miss one, two, three, or even all of the top four needs. To keep from making this mistake, we need to understand the biblical procedure for training Christians.

Second Timothy 3:16 states, "All Scripture is given by inspiration of God, and is profitable for doctrine, for reproof, for correction, for instruction in righteousness." We usually quote this scripture to support the inerrancy of the Bible. But let's look again and see the biblical procedure for training Christians. Four things are needed: doctrine, reproof, correction, and instruction. I don't think it is any accident that Paul lists these four items in this order:

▶ **Doctrine** refers to the norms and standards of the Scriptures. It constitutes the standards by which we must govern our lives and our ministries. Doctrine is not the *process* of teaching but the *product* of teaching.

▶ **Reproof** means showing what is wrong.

▶ **Correction** involves showing what is right.

▶ **Instruction** is simply how-to information and practical application.

Notice how these relate to the spiritual gifts. First, the main ministry of the prophet is pointing out what is wrong, while the main emphasis of the teacher is pointing out what is right. The primary ministry of the exhorter is simply telling how to do it.

We have a tendency to ignore some of these people, most often the prophet. After all, who wants someone stepping on his or her toes and pointing out what's wrong? The prophet makes us uncomfortable. In turn, we keep those who make us uncomfortable out of our lives.

Many churches lack a gifted teacher and a sound doctrinal foundation for their ministry. The person who is doctrine-oriented is usually fact-oriented rather than practical-application-oriented. For that reason, even an outstanding teacher—teaching theology, doctrine, and prophecy week in and week out but without giving much practical application—will have a frustrated congregation.

In addition to doctrine, people need simple, practical, how-to teaching. For instance, consider the man who says, "I know I'm coming up short as a father, but I'm tired of people telling me what I'm doing wrong. I want somebody to show me how to become a better father." On the other hand, you can't teach a man how to be a better father if he doesn't first feel convicted that he *needs* to be a better father. Without conviction, practical teaching will go in one ear and out the other. At the same time, the practical teacher can't be effective if his or her teaching is not based on proper theology, which comes from the gifted teacher.

Some teachers can both bring conviction and explain how-to. Besides teaching, they have the secondary gift of exhortation or prophecy. However, the prophet is usually the one who gets us stirred up or convicted, and the practical exhorter is the one who comes in and gives us the how-to. This type of situation further emphasizes the balance and cooperation that the Bible describes when it deals with spiritual gifts.

Team ministry does not mean exclusiveness. Example: A man comes into your church for help, and the secretary asks, "Are you saved?" He says, "No." So she says, "In that case, you first need to go to the end of the hall and see Rev. Evangelist so he can lead you to Christ. Then you need to go across the hall to see Dr. Teacher so he can show you what's right. After that, you should go upstairs and let Counselor Exhorter show you how to solve your problems." Team ministry involves people who will excel in these different areas of the ministry because of their God-given gifts, but there will always be some overlap in all the areas of giftedness and ministry.

When the right side of the chart is added together, it equals *Team*. The team is a group of Christians empowered by the Holy Spirit. No doubt about it—this is the most powerful force on earth. For years we have let this awesome force lie nearly dormant. Although we have the most powerful force on earth, by doing nothing with it we're letting the world and humanism take over our schools, our government, and the news and entertainment media. As said by Edmund Burke, "All it takes for evil to triumph is for good men to do nothing."

Lasting Growth

When you add all these met needs and active gifts together, you get lasting growth. However, for lasting growth, the church has to meet all these needs in the members' lives. When you miss some of these needs, people are left incomplete. They subconsciously try to fulfill the missing needs. In many cases, they're not even aware the needs exist. All they know is that there's an emptiness in their lives, and they just move on, looking for another church that can meet their needs.

After moving through several churches, such people sometimes drop out completely, thinking that no church can meet their needs. Of course, very few churches can minister perfectly to all these needs. Yet the more needs are met, the more effective the church will be in lasting growth.

The Balance Needed for a Healthy Church

Some churches are strong on outreach. But even though they are getting people saved, many of these converts are simply going out the back door because of an ineffective follow-up program. On the other hand, some churches have good teaching ministries but don't evangelize. The idea is to achieve balance. The balanced church is a growing and healthy church.

In three places where Paul writes on spiritual gifts (Romans 12; 1 Corinthians 12; and Ephesians 4), he uses a five-way analogy of (1) the human body, (2) the Body of Christ, (3) the Church, (4) the members that have, and (5) spiritual gifts. The church is compared to the human body. Members with the various spiritual gifts are compared to the parts of the body. First Corinthians 12:12, 14-15, 17-18, 21-22 (KJV) says,

> For as the body is one, and hath many members, and all the members of that one body, being many, are one body: so also is Christ. . . . For the body is not one member, but many. If the foot shall say, Because I am not the hand, I am not of the body; is it therefore not of the body? . . . If the whole body were an eye, where were the hearing? If the whole were hearing, where were the smelling? But now hath God set the members every one of them in the body, as it hath pleased him. . . . And the eye cannot say unto the hand, I have no need of thee: nor again the head to the feet, I have no need of you. Nay, much more those members of the body, which seem to be more feeble, are necessary.

The question is this: when does the Body of Christ function most effectively and efficiently? When every member is doing what it is supposed to do. When you write with your hands, walk on your feet, hear with your ears, see with your eyes, and all members are working together for one common goal, you are balanced and can function efficiently.

Your responsibility, then, is to equip the laypersons to exercise the spiritual gifts God has given them, in a team effort with the rest of the diversely gifted body, to meet all the needs of every person possible. To develop this effective team, all the gifts must be operating in one local church, thus meeting the needs of all the people in that church or community. We complement each other and meet each other's needs; therefore, we make an effective team.

The "Little Toe" Principle

Some laypersons think, "I know that I'm part of the body, but I'm just the little toe. I'm really not important. I don't have much part in the Body, and I'm not effective at all."

I know a man whose little toe was cut off in an accident. The little toe has much to do with the balance of the body. If a layperson is the little toe in his or her church, he or she has the same effect on the church (the Body of Christ) as this man's little toe had on his body. That layperson is the balance of the church.

The little toe really doesn't have any significant muscles in it. If a person leans off balance and starts to fall, the little toe has no large muscles to stop the person from falling. But it immediately sends a signal to the brain that says, "Out of balance." Then the brain sends a signal to various other muscles to contract to keep the person from falling. My friend without a little toe discovered that if he ran, walked too fast, or simply wasn't paying attention, he would lose his balance and fall.

The worst thing "little toe" laypersons can do is to fall asleep. The little toe that goes to sleep, just like the foot that goes to sleep, affects the whole body. If you have some little-toe people who have fallen asleep on the job, they could be part of what's holding back your church. Therefore, as pastor-coach, make sure you communicate to each team member how much he or she is important to an effectively functioning body.

> I HAVE NEVER HEARD ANYTHING ABOUT THE RESOLUTIONS OF THE DISCIPLES, BUT A GREAT DEAL ABOUT THE ACTS OF THE APOSTLES.
> —HORACE MANN

According to Proverbs 18:15, "The heart of the discerning acquires knowledge, for the ears of the wise seek it out" (NIV). Modeling and encouraging continuing education is one of the key responsibilities of the senior pastor. Harold J. Westing states, "It's only logical that the church staff must model how a team is to function." Purchase good books for your leaders to read. Encourage them to listen to uplifting CDs or podcasts. Send them to seminars.

The more individual church members minister in their areas of gifting, the more balanced the church will be, the more lasting numerical and spiritual growth will take place, and the more God will be honored.

Now in the church that was at Antioch there were certain prophets and teachers: Barnabas, Simeon who was called Niger, Lucius of Cyrene, Manaen who had been brought up with Herod the tetrarch, and Saul. As they ministered to the Lord and fasted, the Holy Spirit said, "Now separate to Me Barnabas and Saul for the work to which I have called them." Then, having fasted and prayed, and laid hands on them, they sent them away (*Acts 13:1–3*).

Oliver Wendell Holmes once wrote, "I find that the great thing is not so much where we stand as in what direction we are moving. To reach the port of heaven we must sail, sometimes with the wind and sometimes against it, but we must sail and not drift, nor lie at anchor."

We've talked about the importance of lay ministry teams. We've also seen the role of the pastor-coach in the success of the teams. But there comes a time when we must move from the strategy session to the playing field.

Marlene Wilson writes about moving to that playing field:

To get pewsitters moving, the pastor can do several things. Interview new members to discover their strengths and gifts. Define leadership goals. If members and potential leaders know what to expect in leadership roles, they won't be scared away by the fear of too little knowledge or too much responsibility. Teach a team approach that allows everyone to contribute their strengths and weakness, concerns and dreams. Encourage natural leaders while making sure that unnatural leaders aren't forced into leadership roles.[1]

In an interview with David Frost, General Norman Schwarzkopf, the commander of the Allied forces in the Gulf War, was asked, "What's the greatest lesson you've learned out of all this?" Schwarzkopf replied,

> I think there is one really fundamental military truth. And that's that you can add up the correlation of forces, you can look at the number of tanks, you can look at the number of airplanes, you can look at all these factors of military might and put them together. But unless the soldier on the ground, or the airman in the air, has the will to win, has the strength of character to go into the battle, believes that his cause is just, and has the support of his country—all the rest of that stuff is irrelevant.

The same is true of church ministry teams. Without each person's conviction that the cause is worth the price, the battle will never be won, and the team will not succeed. There must be commitment. We must get the team onto the playing field!

However, a 1993 Gallup poll of religion in America found that fifty percent of church members are unwilling to do anything for the church, forty percent are just waiting to be asked, and only ten percent are presently involved in the church's ministry. Certainly these percentages will have to dramatically change if the Church in America is going to have the impact God intends for it to have. Ministry Action Teams are the answer. It's time to include and empower the forty percent who are waiting to be asked.

HOW TO ENSURE SUCCESSFUL MINISTRY ACTION TEAMS

When you have educated and gift-tested your congregation, you are free to begin establishing your Ministry Action Teams. But before the teams are fully established, the team members and the pastor-coach must understand the four distinct phases in a person's growth toward participation in the church's ministry:

1. Assimilation. In assimilation a person comes to understand how to become a part of the local church.

2. Teaching. Those who are assimilated into the church should be taught the biblical basis for lay ministry.

3. Development. Through gift testing and personality profiles, church members will begin to discover their spiritual gifts and callings.

4. Placement. The ultimate goal is for every member to become a minister in some capacity.

Not only must a church member grow from initial assimilation to actual placement in the church's ministry, the pastor's role must also "grow" through different phases. As the church grows, the pastor's hands-on ministry will decrease, while the congregation's hands-on ministry must increase. And this hands-on ministry will be done most effectively by teams of people with diverse knowledge and skills, not by those who are just "clones" of the pastor.

> WHEN INSTITUTIONS EMERGE, THE FOCUS TENDS TO SHIFT RATHER QUICKLY FROM THE MOVERS AND THE MOVEMENT TO THE MACHINE AND THE MONUMENTS.
> —ROBERT DALE

MEETING THE NEEDS OF TEAM MEMBERS

In his book *Team Building: An Exercise in Leadership* Robert B. Maddux lists seven things that a team member needs from the coach in order to be effective:

1. A basic understanding of his or her job and its contribution to the team
2. A continuing understanding of what is expected from him or her
3. The opportunity to participate in planning change and to perform in keeping with team abilities
4. The opportunity to receive assistance when needed
5. Feedback to know how well he or she is doing
6. Recognition and reward based on his or her performance
7. The right work in a climate that encourages self-development.[2]

Not only must the coach firmly apply those principles in the establishment of the Ministry Action Teams, but also the team members themselves must embrace what I call "The Heavenly Seven."

The Heavenly Seven

1. Show love for one another.
2. Inform one another.
3. Learn as a group.
4. Acknowledge ministry gifts.
5. Have "the attitude of Christ."
6. Be committed to the cause of Christ.
7. Celebrate victories together.

MOVING TO THE MINISTRY
ACTION TEAM PHILOSOPHY

Any time a church attempts a move from one ministry philosophy to another, some fundamental issues will be raised.

Issue No. 1: Inclusion (Who is on the team?)

Issue No. 2: Direction (Who is in charge?)

Issue No. 3: Affection (How much trust is there?)

Issue No. 4: Implementation (How will we achieve our goals?)

Building a team is not like making instant coffee; it is more of a "brewing" process. It takes time and requires patience by both the coach and the players. The process is not as blissful as some may lead you to believe. In fact, many churches have tried Ministry Action Teams and have seen them "stumble at the gate."

An effective Ministry Action Team, however, will view the growth process realistically. For example, in the initial year of shifting to Ministry Action Team activities, there is often a tentativeness. It is easy for discouragement and frustration to set in if only a few tangible results are seen right away. Understanding the following distinct stages of ministry team development and the possible "growing pains" inherent to each stage will help to head off discouragement:

- ► *Forming* (getting organized for team ministry)
- ► *Storming* (brainstorming, coming up with ideas, creating vision)
- ► *Norming* (establishing a consistent pattern of ministry)
- ► *Performing* (working in the power of the Holy Spirit)

Now all who believed were together, and had all things in common, and sold their possessions and goods, and divided them among all, as anyone had need. So continuing daily with one accord in the temple, and breaking bread from house to house, they ate their food with gladness and simplicity of heart, praising God and having favor with all the people. And the Lord added to the church daily those who were being saved (*Acts 2:44–47*).

THE APPOINTMENT OF THE APOSTOLIC TEAM

He went up on the mountain and called to Him those He Himself wanted. And they came to Him. Then He appointed twelve, that they might be with Him and that He might send them out to preach, and to have power to heal sicknesses and to cast out demons: Simon, to whom He gave the name Peter; James the son of Zebedee and John the brother of James, to whom He gave the name Boanerges, that is, "Sons of Thunder"; Andrew, Philip, Bartholomew, Matthew, Thomas, James the son of Alphaeus, Thaddaeus, Simon the Canaanite; and Judas Iscariot, who also betrayed Him. And they went into a house (*Mark 3:13–19*).

THE SEVEN ACTIONS OF IMPLEMENTATION

Implementing a team ministry involves seven distinct actions:

1. Developing the dream for Kingdom-building
2. Structuring the team for comprehensive ministry
3. Establishing the role of each team leader
4. Communicating vital information to the entire team
5. Permitting the team to innovate and create
6. Recognizing the weaknesses inherent in all human beings
7. Releasing the team to do ministry in Jesus' name

LAUNCHING YOUR MINISTRY ACTION TEAMS

Dodger great Tommy Lasorda once said, "My responsibility is to get my twenty-five guys playing for the name on the front of their uniform and not the one on the back." Merging the gifts and personalities of individuals into a cohesive team is no small challenge, but with God's help it can be done. Let me suggest nine steps for launching your team.

Step 1: Determine Your Ministry Areas

You may want to categorize the entire ministry of your church into separate areas. For example—Christian education, building and maintenance, worship, fellowship, evangelism, and so forth. (See the seven Ministry Action Teams in chapter 6.) Ministry Action Teams may be appointed to supervise the ongoing ministries in those areas.

Teams for those ministry areas should be recruited and appointed on the basis of their skills and interests in those areas.

Step 2: Structure Your Team

How many members will be on the team? How long will the team serve? What is the main function of the team? These are among the questions that will be answered in a written job description that you will prepare for your team. Good delegation begins with good direction.

Chris Russell offers this excellent advice:

Remember that it's best to delegate responsibilities rather than specific tasks. That way, you can provide general directions without having to keep assigning new tasks. Be sure the person has the authority to carry out the delegated responsibility. He or she must have the power to make decisions within the parameters you establish. Realize that it's not bad for lay people to make mistakes. As long as it's not the same mistake over and over, it shows that they're learning, growing, and trying new things.[3]

Step 3: Evaluate Potential Team Members

As has been said, each team member is unique. Ability levels will differ. Temperaments will differ. Personalities will differ. The skilled coach will see how those unique individuals may work together as a team. As a rule, however, potential teammates should have at least some degree of compatibility.

Of course, the first ingredient in structuring a team is prayer. God's Word promises, "If any of you lacks wisdom, let him ask of God, who gives to all liberally and without reproach, and it will be given to him" (James 1:5). Since He created them, God knows our potential team members far better than we ever will. He knows exactly which person belongs on your team.

Step 4: Choose Leaders

Red Auerbach, the legendary Boston Celtics coach, once remarked, "How you select people is more important than how you manage them once they are on the job." According to Bobb Biehl, having the right players determines sixty to eighty percent of the success of any organization. And having the right leaders is just as important! Choosing solid team leaders is one of the most crucial steps in creating exceptional Ministry Action Teams. One of the characteristics of an effective coach is the ability to spot good players. Paul modeled this trait in the case of Timothy: "Then he [Paul] came to Derbe and Lystra. And behold, a certain disciple was there, named Timothy, the son of a certain Jewish woman who believed, but his father was Greek. He was well spoken of by the brethren who were at Lystra and Iconium. Paul wanted to have him go on with him" (Acts 16:1–3).

It is wonderful to be a naturally good trainer and to have a knack for picking potential leaders. But Jesus took it a step further. Before He engaged in training, He first spent all night in prayer, making sure He was picking just the right leaders: "Now it came to pass in those days that He went out to the mountain to pray, and continued all night in prayer to God. And when it was day, He called His disciples to Himself; and from them He chose twelve whom He also named apostles" (Luke 6:12–13).

The twelve men Jesus chose for His team seemed destined for calamity, but He saw their potential. Although it appeared highly unlikely those twelve diverse men would be able to work together as a harmonious team, by Acts 2:1 they were all with one accord in one place. Jesus had molded them into a functional team. (But remember that they had their failures along the way—even to the point of deserting Jesus during the crucifixion experience. Don't despair when you see failure!)

Don Cousins shares four important steps to use in selecting the right players to lead the teams:

Strength of Character. Nothing is more important! This involves traits such as discipline, honesty, teachability, humility, trustworthiness, and dependability.

Spiritual Authenticity. Does the person have a heart that is fully the Lord's? Does he or she have a vital devotional life and share their faith with others? "For the eyes of the Lord run to and fro throughout the whole earth, to show Himself strong on behalf of those whose heart is loyal to Him" (2 Chronicles 16:9).

Ministry Fit. What people do should reflect who they are—their spiritual gifts, temperament, passion, personality, and background.

Team Fit. Team members who like each other and benefit from being around each other will work well together and bear much fruit.

In *Developing the Leaders Around You,* John C. Maxwell says that when he chooses leaders, he looks for people who—

1. Know his heart, which takes time.
2. Are loyal to him, for they are an extension of him and his work.
3. Are trustworthy, not abusing authority, power, or confidences.
4. Are discerning, for they make decisions for him.
5. Have a servant's heart, for they will carry a heavy load.
6. Are good thinkers, for two heads are better than one.
7. Are able to follow through, taking authority and carrying out the vision.

8. Have a great heart for God, for that is the driving force in Maxwell's own life.[4]

Step 5: Form the Team

Church researcher George Barna reports that one out of every four adults—twenty-four percent—volunteer their free time to participate in the life of the church. Mobilizing this great volunteer army in skilled teams is key to the success of the local church.

Some important procedures should be considered when forming your teams:

- ▸ Give everyone a chance.
- ▸ Make clear ministry assignments.
- ▸ Form ministry objectives that can be measured.
- ▸ Delegate with permission to fail.
- ▸ Demand accountability at every level of ministry.
- ▸ Evaluate and refine frequently. (Ministry plans should be tested against the overall vision plan of the church.)
- ▸ Be ready to make adjustments.
- ▸ Determine to persevere.

Step 6: Provide Adequate Training

Military leaders wouldn't think of sending their troops into battle without proper training. Neither should church leaders. In order to be prepared for their ministry assignments, laypersons need adequate training times. "What king, going to make war against another king, does not sit down first and consider whether he is able with ten thousand to meet him who comes against him with twenty thousand?" (Luke 14:31).

By virtue of its schedules, the local church has built-in training times. Sunday School, midweek services, pre-service classes, and other opportunities can be turned into "basic training" sites for Ministry Action Team recruits. Resistance to breaking the traditional structures can be overcome by laying a thorough groundwork in teaching the entire congregation the importance of the teams and their biblical mandate.

The training times may include audiovisual presentations, class assignments, guest lectures, discussion times, informal refreshment times, and, of course, on-the-job practice. Every effort should be made to make the training sessions professional yet personal.

The pastor-coach never knows what potential ministry standout may be in the class. *The Free Methodist* magazine gave these examples:

1. A six-year-old lad came home with a note from his teacher in which it was suggested that he be taken out of school, as he was "too stupid to learn." That boy was Thomas A. Edison.

2. Alfred Tennyson's grandfather gave him ten shillings for writing his grandmother's eulogy. Handing it to the lad, the old man said, "There—that is the first money you ever earned by your poetry, and take my word for it: it will be the last."

3. Benjamin Franklin's mother-in-law hesitated at letting her daughter marry a printer. There were already two printing offices in the United States, and she feared that the country might not be able to support a third.

Step 7: Publicly Recognize Appointees

The completion of the training sessions is a wonderful time to give a public recognition of the appointment and the training efforts of your Ministry Action Team. Everyone loves a celebration! A Sunday evening worship service, for instance, could include a presentation of the biblical mandate for ministry and a commissioning of the team. The service may also be a wonderful time to present the plan of salvation to guests of the team who have been invited to the commissioning service.

In his book *Sources of Strength*, former President Jimmy Carter recalled his walk down Pennsylvania Avenue with his family members following his inauguration. Carter's mother was instructed not to stop for reporters' questions, but she ignored the advice and responded to a reporter who asked, "Miss Lillian, aren't you proud of your son?"

The president said his mother replied, "Which one?"

Certainly your Ministry Action Team should understand that the "ground is level at the foot of the Cross"—that we have all been adopted into the same body. But a little recognition for the commitment and the efforts of team members will serve them well when the ministry load gets heavy and times of discouragement set in. They may look back to their commissioning service as a point of reference.

Paul encouraged the Church to give recognition to those who earn it: "Render therefore to all their due: taxes to whom taxes are due, customs to whom customs, fear to whom fear, honor to whom honor" (Romans 13:7).

Step 8: Release the Team for Ministry

A Baptist church set its sights on a well-known down-and-outer in the community. They repeatedly invited the man to church, but he refused their invitation, saying he didn't have good-enough clothes to wear.

Finally, some of the members of the church decided to do something about his clothes excuse. They invited him to the neighborhood department store and bought him a beautiful new suit, shirt, tie, and shoes. "There!" The proud committee said "We'll be looking for you this Sunday."

Sunday came, and there was no sign of the man with the new clothes. The pastor spotted him the next week and asked him why he didn't come to church. "Well, the truth is, Reverend," the man answered, "I looked in the mirror and saw how good I looked—and decided to go to First Presbyterian!"

Your Ministry Action Team may be well-dressed, well-trained, and well-recognized, but the time comes when they must be released for ministry in their appointed areas. The awful tendency in some churches is to spend too much time in training and not enough time in implementation.

The pastor-coach has already given the team "assignment with authority." Team members know they have the authority to minister within the parameters of their job description. Now it's time to send the team out of the locker room and onto the playing field.

Pastor-coaches must resist the urge to micromanage. Ministry Action Team leaders should be given plenty of time and space for team leaders to do the job without feeling paranoid. They must learn to persevere in the "heat of the battle."

Og Mandino gives a great example of what can happen with perseverance. He tells the story of Raphael Solano and his companions who were looking for diamonds in a dry river bed. Discouraged, Solano claimed he had picked up about 999,999 rocks and was quitting. His companions said, "Pick up one more and make it a million." That millionth rock was "The Liberator," the largest and purest diamond ever found. Mandino writes, "I think he (Solano) must have known a happiness that went beyond the financial. He had set his course; the odds were against him; he had persevered; he had won. He had not only done what he had set out to do—which is a reward in itself—but he had done it in the face of failure and obscurity."[5]

Step 9: Conduct a Debriefing Session

After the Ministry Action Team completes its first assignment, it's time to bring them back together for a reporting time. This is a good place to discuss fears, failures, and triumphs in a nonthreatening environment.

It's also a good time for a pat on the back for a job "well tried." We all like to have our efforts appreciated. The encouragement you offer your team after its first assignment could well set the tone for all of its future endeavors.

It was President Gerald Ford who signed a bill posthumously promoting George Washington to the rank of six-star general. Congress had awarded the rank for the man who would become the first president in a bill passed March 3, 1799, but then-President John Adams never got around to submitting Washington's name to the Senate for confirmation.

An effective pastor-coach or team leader is always current in the appreciation department!

UNDERSTANDING MINISTRY PRIORITIES

Consider this pastoral search committee report:

In our search for a suitable pastor, the following scratch sheet was developed for your perusal. Of the candidates investigated by the committee, only one was found to have the necessary qualities. The list contains the names of the candidates and comments on each, should you be interested in investigating them further for future pastoral placements:

Noah: Has 120 years of preaching experience, but no converts.

Moses: Stutters, and his former congregation says he loses his temper over trivial things.

Abraham: Took off to Egypt during hard times. We heard that he got into trouble with the authorities and then tried to lie his way out.

David: Has an unacceptable moral character. He might have been considered for minister of music had he not fallen.

Solomon: Has a reputation for wisdom but fails to practice what he preaches.

Elijah: Proved to be inconsistent and is known to fold under pressure.

Hosea: His family life is in a shambles. Divorced and remarried to a prostitute.

Jeremiah: He is too emotional, an alarmist; some say a real pain in the neck.

Amos: Comes from a farming background. Better off picking figs.

John: Says he is a Baptist but lacks tact and dresses like a hippie. Would not feel comfortable at a church potluck supper.

Peter: Has a bad temper and was heard to have even denied Christ publicly.

Paul: We found him to lack tact. He is too harsh, his appearance is contemptible, and he preaches far too long.

Timothy: He has potential but is much too young for the position.

Jesus: Tends to offend church members with his preaching, especially Bible scholars. He is also too controversial. He even offended the search committee with his pointed questions.

Judas: Seemed to be very practical, cooperative, good with money, cares for the poor, and dresses well. We all agreed that he is just the man we are looking for to fill the vacancy as our senior pastor.

Thank you for all you have done in assisting us with our pastoral search.

Sincerely,

The Pastoral Search Committee

While this search committee might rank as the toughest one ever, a pastor-coach who understands how to prioritize ministry in the local church will always rank high in the minds of its leaders.

Baseball legend Babe Ruth was asked how he always came through in the clutch—how he could step up to bat with the game on the line in the bottom of the ninth and hit the ball for a game-winning run.

Ruth answered in the simplest terms, "I just keep my eye on the ball."

Game-winning ministry focuses on priorities. And the first priority is to seek first the kingdom of God and His righteousness (Matthew 6:33).

The following vital areas deserve top priority for establishing Ministry Action Teams:

Ministry context. The church family must understand why pastors do what they do.

Factors affecting ministry success. All obstacles should be dealt with before leading ministry teams.

Action plans. Ministry team members must have a voice in the development of key strategies.

Communication channels. Clear lines of information must be established.

Implementation stages and schedules. There should be specific target and scheduling deadlines for implementing team ministry.

Monitoring, review, and evaluation. An evaluation form should be created to monitor and review the progress of ministry teams.

THE LEADERSHIP LEGACY OF JOHN WOODEN

Coach John Wooden's UCLA Bruins basketball team won an astonishing eighty-eight games in a row, thirty-six consecutive playoff games, and ten national championships. Citing teamwork as the key to victory, Wooden offers the following acrostic:

T—ogether. We need to work together rather than as individuals.

E—mpathy. We need empathy for all the team members.

A—ssist. We need to assist in helping others.

M—aturity. We need maturity in order to handle problems.

W—illingness. We need to be willing to work together in harmony.

O—rganization. We need proper organization in order to have a smooth operation.

R—espect. We need respect for the coach and the other team members.

K—indness. We need kindness for everyone we come into contact with.

Furthermore, John Wooden always stressed that "a team is a group of people working together for a common purpose." A group of people who do not know their common purpose is not a team—even though they may call themselves a team. A true team knows its calling. Just as John Wooden's philosophy brought measurable results on the basketball court, so teamwork in the church will bring tangible results—growth upon growth.

> **NONPROFIT ORGANIZATIONS FIND IT VERY HARD TO ANSWER THE QUESTION "WHAT, THEN, ARE THE RESULTS IN OUR INSTITUTION?"**
> —PETER DRUCKER

▷ Team-building Tips

- ▸ Cross-train team leaders in a myriad of ministry skills.
- ▸ Create common expectations and understandings for all team members.
- ▸ Eliminate the duplication of ministry team endeavors.
- ▸ Use consensus decision-making to establish team priorities.
- ▸ Celebrate the "special days" of your teammates.
- ▸ Evaluate team effectiveness.
- ▸ Hold team leaders accountable for decisions made.
- ▸ Ask for positive statements from negative teammates.
- ▸ Show respect for team members' families.
- ▸ Incorporate goals with appraisals.
- ▸ Give paid pastoral staff an annual salary increase based on team performance.
- ▸ Conduct a round-robin meeting to collect team ministry ideas.

▷ Resource Tip
Developing Interpersonal Skills

Implementing Ministry Action Teams in any local church will require change, and managing that change calls for a high degree of relational skill. Learn the secrets of managing change well from *Five Secrets of an Exceptional Leader,* by Stan Toler.

5

FINE-TUNE MINISTRY ACTION TEAMS

WE THEN, AS WORKERS TOGETHER WITH HIM ALSO PLEAD
WITH YOU NOT TO RECEIVE THE GRACE OF GOD IN VAIN.
—2 CORINTHIANS 6:1

▲

My college basketball coach, David Lattimer, was one of the most effective coaches I have ever played for. Coach Lattimer understood the strengths and weaknesses of every team member. He understood that my brother, Terry, was a great shooter and playmaker. He also knew that I was a baseball player wearing basketball clothes! Often when he sent me into the game he would say, "Stan, remember two things: First, find the leading scorer and foul him till you foul out! Don't let him come into our house and act this way! And, second, whatever you do, don't shoot . . . uh . . . unless they give you a free throw. But be careful!" Frankly, at first I didn't understand why I wasn't allowed to shoot like my brother, Terry. However, I ultimately realized that my role was very valuable to the team. I was never on the court long, but I was important because I stopped some great plays by the opposing team. At last I realized that I was an effective contributor to a winning team!

CELEBRATE UNIQUENESS

Legendary basketball player Bill Walton said, "In basketball, you may be the greatest player in the world and lose every game, because a team will always beat an individual." The church ministry team is God's instrument in meeting the needs of people in your community as well as in your church. Your responsibility as pastor-coach is to encourage laypersons to exercise the spiritual gifts God has given them in a team effort to meet those needs.

Coach Lattimer obviously recognized my limited abilities and found the best spot for me on the team. Likewise, if church teams are to be successful, the pastor-coach must encourage the team to be enthusiastic about their unique talents and their specialized areas of ministry.

DEFINE SUCCESS IN PRACTICAL TERMS

It is not what laypersons are that holds them back but what they think they aren't. Many laypersons live way below their potential. Others are living up to their potential but have such low self-esteem that they don't acknowledge it. They are much more successful than they think they are.

The task of the pastor-coach is to develop the potential of ministry team members by making them aware of what true success really is. "Successful" people are those who have found God's will and are living in it to the best of their abilities. It has been wisely said, "To know God's will is the greatest knowledge; to do God's will is the greatest achievement."

When a pastor has a congregation who is doing God's will, it will be easier to recruit Ministry Action Team members. Since the local church is somewhat like a business corporation, Glenn M. Parker's characteristics of a successful corporate team in his book *Team Players and Teamwork* are highly relevant. They are—

Clear purpose. The vision, mission, goal, or task of the team has been defined and is now accepted by everyone. The mission statement has been followed up with an action plan.

Informality. The climate tends to be informal, comfortable, and relaxed, with no obvious tensions or signs of boredom.

Participation. There is much discussion, and everyone is encouraged to be involved.

Listening. The members use effective listening techniques such as questioning, paraphrasing, and summarizing to get ideas.

Civilized disagreement. There is disagreement, but the team is comfortable with it and shows no signs of avoiding, smoothing over, or suppressing conflict.

Consensus decision-making. For important decisions the goal is substantial, but not necessarily unanimous, agreement. This is based on an open discussion of everyone's ideas and avoids formal voting or easy compromise.

Open communication. Team members feel free to express their feelings on the tasks as well as on the group's operation. There are few hidden agendas. Communication takes place both inside and outside meetings.

Clear roles and assignments. There are clear expectations about the roles played by each team member. When action is taken, clear assignments are made, accepted, and carried out. Work is fairly distributed among team members.

Shared leadership. While the team has a formal leader, leadership functions shift from time to time depending upon the circumstances, the needs of the group, and the skills of the members. The formal leader models the appropriate behavior and helps establish positive norms.

External relations. The team spends time developing key outside relationships, mobilizing resources, and building credibility with important players in other parts of the organization.

Style diversity. The team has a broad spectrum of team-player types.

Self-assessment. Periodically the team stops to examine how well it is functioning and what may be interfering with its effectiveness.[1]

Trying to reverse the American buyer's trend toward purchasing imports, the Ford Motor Company made a bold move. A mid-sized car was designed and manufactured in a brand-new way. Traditionally, Ford designers made sketches and passed them on to manufacturing departments. For years designers etched out sketches that were passed on to manufacturing departments. Sales received the finished product and had to figure out a way to sell it.

This time a team was put together to handle the project from ground zero. Department heads were assembled and asked to make a wish list for an ideal car. From that point on, the manufacturing team worked to carry out the wishes of the vision-casting team. The result was one of the best-selling Ford products ever. More than one million units of the award-winning Taurus were sold in the first four years.

Working alone, those individual experts could not succeed. But working as a team, those same gifted individuals wonderfully accomplished their goal. Why? In Bill Walton's words, "Because a team will always beat an individual."

LOOK FOR THE KEY INGREDIENTS

Bottom Line magazine lists key ingredients that all successful teams have in common.[2]

Shared purpose. First, the leader instills a shared sense of purpose. Ray Stato, chairman of Analog Devices Line, says, "The leader must create a sense of purpose, clarity of vision, and a conviction that the individuals of the team are world-class." Synergy is created when each team member shares the team's vision.

Team goals. Second, all goals become team goals. Unless the whole team wins, no one wins! Individual accomplishments are fine for the record books, but they're really an afterthought. The Boston Celtics won sixteen NBA championships and never once had the league-leading scorer on their team. Good leaders speak in the first-person plural: "We need . . ." "Our deadline . . ." "The job before us . . ."

Individual freedom. Third, individuality is celebrated. Team-work doesn't discount individuality. Everyone has a unique personality, differing skills, and definitive hopes and fears. Olympian Mary Lou Retton once said, "A talented leader will remember those differences, appreciate them, and use them to the advantage of the team."

Shared responsibility. Fourth, personal as well as corporate responsibility is shared. Projects belong to the team. Solutions may bubble up from the group, and that participation should be welcomed. But dictated or imposed decisions shouldn't come from the top. The team must solve the problem.

Shared glory and acceptance of blame. Fifth, shared glory is accompanied by acceptance of blame. When the team does well, the whole team benefits. Share the glory, whether by a public pat on the back, a bonus, or a write-up in the church newsletter. Whatever form recognition takes, every team member should get a generous share of it. Al Abrour, former coach of the New York Islanders, used to say about his coaching style, "I praise in public, criticize in private."

Confidence-building. Sixth, confidence-building is a continuous endeavor. A great leader believes firmly in the team. When a leader is always communicating positive confidence toward the team, a feeling develops among the teammates that they don't want to disappoint the leader or the group.

> THE AVERAGE PASTOR SPENDS OVER TEN HOURS A WEEK GOING TO MEETINGS. THE AVERAGE CONGREGATION SPENDS NINETY PEOPLE-HOURS CONSIDERING WHETHER OR NOT TO START A NEW MINISTRY, ONLY TO SAY NO TO MOST OF THEM.
>
> —WILLIAM EASUM

A Game Plan for Success

- ▸ Develop a formula for winning.
- ▸ Position people for success.
- ▸ Focus on victory.
- ▸ Adjust today so you can win tomorrow.

SOLVE PROBLEMS TOGETHER

One of the most important functions of highly effective teams is to find direction and solve problems—together. Teams can best find answers to problems by using a simple eight-step process:

1. Discuss the history of the situation.
2. Establish a plan of action.
3. Determine potential pitfalls.
4. Dialogue about possible methods.
5. Ask, "What will be the most effective path?"
6. Share information with the team.
7. Get started immediately!
8. Monitor and review the results.

Robert B. Maddux urges that problem-solving techniques be taught at every level of the organization. He recommends the following process.[3]

State the apparent problem. First, state what *appears* to be the problem. The real problem may not surface until facts have been gathered and analyzed. Therefore, start with a supposition that can later be confirmed or corrected.

Gather information. Next, gather facts, feelings, and opinions. What happened? Where, when, and how did it occur? What is the "real" size, scope, and severity of the problem? Who is affected by it? Is it likely to happen again? Does it really need to be corrected? Time and expense may require problem-solvers to think through the actual need and assign priorities to the more critical elements.

Restate the problem. Then restate the problem, reiterating the facts that may provide supporting data. The actual problem may or may not be the same as the one identified at the beginning.

Identify solutions. Next, identify alternative solutions. Generate ideas. Do not eliminate any possible solutions until several have been discussed.

Evaluate alternatives. Which alternatives will provide the optimum solution? What are the risks? Are the costs in keeping with the benefits? Will the solution create new problems?

Implement the decision. Then move to action. Who must be involved? To what extent? How, when, and where? Whom will the decision impact? What might go wrong? How will results be reported and verified?

Evaluate the results. Finally, test the solution against the desired results. Modify the solution if better results are needed.

MODEL THE BEST OF THE BEST

A good example of highly effective Ministry Action Teams comes from the Glasgow Reformed Presbyterian Church. That church uses evangelism teams based in house churches as their primary tool for reaching the lost. In order to do this, they have developed two specific teams.

1. Acquaintance-making Events

Acquaintance-making Events, called AMEs for short, are held for the purpose of introducing unchurched friends to other church members. These events usually take place in larger groups (more than eight) and never one-on-one. They are planned ahead of time and organized. AMEs are social gatherings such as picnics, cookouts, parties, hospitality events, and afternoon teas. They usually take place outside the church. Their purpose is simple: to help develop a three-way relationship or friendship bridge among the church member, his or her invited unsaved and unchurched friend, and the regular members of the group. When planning AMEs, laypersons must remember four basic rules.

1. Be sure to invite unsaved and unchurched friends every time the group has a social function.
2. Be careful about being too pushy.
3. Be sure to mingle, and do not ignore the newcomers.
4. Be patient.

2. Relationship-strengthening Activities

Relationship-strengthening Activities, or RSAs, are activities for the purpose of developing, cultivating, strengthening, and building trusting relationships between unchurched friends and church members. These activities usually take place in smaller groups (four or fewer), or even one-on-one. RSAs are more informal than AMEs in the sense that they are less planned, more spontaneous, and may include activities such as shopping trips, dining out, or watching a game on television. When involved in RSAs, laypersons must avoid being on the edge of their seats all evening looking for the perfect time to twist the conversation into a presentation of the gospel. Instead, they should allow God to open the opportunity at the natural time. Be a good witness at all times in entertainment, conduct, and dress. Don't condemn or belittle the friends' lifestyles.

This approach keeps individual Christians from having to go it alone in their efforts to fulfill the Great Commission. The group works together as an evangelism team to support each other, pray for their lost friends, and create the environment of friendship needed to introduce newcomers to Christ and His Church. Acquaintance-making Events and Relationship-strengthening Activities are great ways for bringing the seeker and the nonseeker into the church's sphere of influence.

LEARN FROM THE AMERICA'S CUP TEAM

The America's Cup yachting challenge pits the world's top sailors against the forces of nature, exacting from them their greatest efforts as they represent their various countries. Without a crew, the finest yacht-building efforts would be to no avail. The ship simply can't sail by itself. And without a skipper, the crew would lack the direction necessary to carry out their task.

Such is the case with the pastor-coach and team ministry. As with the AME and RSA outreach ministries mentioned, pastors need laypersons to bring their friends to church to hear the sermons they've prepared. Similarly, laypersons need pastors to preach those sermons to the friends they've brought to church. Pastor and laypersons (skipper and crew) need to work together. Good coordinated teamwork is the key to effective church ministry.

As a yachting captain encourages the crew to their ultimate performance, so pastor-coaches must take the initiative to mold their congregation into an excellent ministry team. In turn, the pastor-coach must be willing to accept God's molding to best meet the needs of the congregation.

TROUBLESHOOTING

Michael Costa, the celebrated conductor, was holding a rehearsal. As the mighty chorus rang out, accompanied by scores of instruments, the piccolo player thought he could quit playing without being missed since there was so much music being played. Suddenly the great leader stopped and cried out, "Where is the piccolo?" The sound of that one small instrument was necessary for the full harmony of the musical score, and the skilled conductor's ear had missed it when it did not play. So it is with your congregation. Every part—including your own—must be played, and played in tune, or the whole congregation will suffer.

But what if a part is played out of tune or not played at all because of dissension? All your hard work as a pastor-coach could be in jeopardy. Sometimes a shift to team-building can be going very smoothly only to be destroyed by internal problems. Wise leaders will be on the alert to these barriers of team ministry success. Preventive medicine is always the best policy. Effective ministry team leaders never wait until things are at a critical impasse before they take action. Watch for these signs of trouble, and offer remedies so that obstacles to success can be overcome before they harm your church's ministry.

WATCH FOR DANGER SIGNS

A good team leader must be able to recognize symptoms of trouble within the group. Tim Rudlaff offers the following ten signs that your team has underlying difficulties that need to be addressed.[4]

1. Meetings become formal and tense. Be concerned if team members seem not to be relaxed during meeting times. Team players should be creative and dynamic when they are together. *Remedy*: Open all meetings with prayer, icebreakers, and a humorous story.

2. Teammates participate but don't achieve. When team members start enjoying social interaction but fail to get much accomplished, it is a warning sign. *Remedy*: Appoint a team leader who is a doer.

3. Teammates talk but don't communicate. Some people don't want to listen—they only want to talk. Team communications should be an interactive give-and-take. *Remedy*: Ask the team to summarize what has been said. Appoint a team scribe to write down vital information that has been shared.

4. Disputes are resolved in private after team meetings. Healthy teams have open discussions about their differences. Private discussions of team matters quickly build distrust. *Remedy*: Feedback should be shared only when the entire team is present.

5. The team leader makes most decisions. This can happen if the leader is too aggressive or the team members are too quiet. Every member needs to contribute—that's why it's called a team. *Remedy*: Ask the team leader to keep a list of those involved in the process and share it with the senior pastor on a monthly basis.

6. Teammates don't trust each other. When a team is starting, this can be expected. However, lack of trust is a serious problem. *Remedy*: Appoint only trustworthy leaders.

7. There is confusion about ministry roles. Whenever there are misunderstandings or conflicts about assignments, things need to be clarified quickly. *Remedy*: Distribute copies of all ministry job descriptions.

8. Teammates publicly embarrass or criticize others. If legitimate feedback or criticism needs to be discussed, it must be done in private—never in front of other team members. *Remedy*: Confront the team leaders with care and concern. Emphasize the importance of esteeming the ministry team members.

9. Things promised are not delivered. This generally indicates mistrust or a spirit of carelessness toward the team, and it wears down morale. *Remedy*: Establish accountability lines, and ask for periodic updates.

10. Confidences are broken. This causes team members to lose respect for one another. They will become reluctant to talk for fear of what their teammates will do with the information. *Remedy*: Find a new team leader quickly!

In Him you also trusted, after you heard the word of truth, the gospel of your salvation; in whom also, having believed, you were sealed with the Holy Spirit of promise, who is the guarantee of our inheritance until the redemption of the purchased possession, to the praise of His glory. Therefore I also, after I heard of your faith in the Lord Jesus and your love for all the saints, do not cease to give thanks for you, making mention of you in my prayers; that the God of our Lord Jesus Christ, the Father of glory, may give to you the spirit of wisdom and revelation in the knowledge of Him (*Ephesians 1:13–17*).

AVOID GIFT-IMPOSING

Gift-imposing is the act of forcing your own spiritual gift upon another person and attempting to compel that person to perform it as though it were his or her gift. For example, gift-imposers want the whole body to be an "eye"—or whatever member they may be. Such individuals fail to recognize the diversity of the Body of Christ and as a result force other Christians to function in capacities for which God has not gifted them.

Gift-imposers give the impression that the area of ministry for which God has gifted and burdened them is superior to all others. In fact, some not only subtly give that impression but also openly declare that their gifts are the only ones that count. They may even determine that there is only one gift—and that gift belongs to them. Gift-imposers distribute much frustration, discouragement, and false guilt among others on the ministry team.

Gift-imposers also use guilt trips to force their gifts on others. They try to make others feel that they are not right with God unless they are involved with the same ministry as they are. For example, some people have the gift of evangelism. They are motivated and consumed with personally leading people to Christ. They witness with tracts and confront people on the street, in doctors' offices, on the bus—anywhere and anytime they can. When they find fellow Christians with another gift—the gift of serving or the gift of mercy, for instance—and see those people are not out on the streets witnessing as they are, the evangelist accuses them of not being "burdened for souls."

In reality, that evangelist's assessment may be far from the truth. Someone with the gift of mercy may actually have been responsible for many coming to Christ. And the server may have opened doors the evangelist could only have wished to open. No believer who uses his or her gift properly should feel guilty for not having the same gift as someone else.

Gift-imposers work in two basic ways: first, they try to convince others of their great burden; second, they try to convince others by repeating their message—they become one-string banjos, restating the same theme week in and week out. This drives many potential workers away and makes those workers who stay think the gift-imposer's gift or ministry is all there is.

The remedy for this condition is to speak with the person who is imposing his or her gift on others. The following advice is good for both the gift-imposer as well as the person who may feel imposed upon:

We all have heroes in the work of God, people we consider great and outstanding because of their positions and accomplishments. But God has called each individual to do something unique. The church needs the manifestation of each gift. You are accountable for the gift God has given you—not for God's calling on someone else's life.

In order for the gift-imposer to understand his or her unique place in ministry, the pastor-coach may want to help that individual understand several important principles of gift use:

► Do what God has called you to do.

► Make your personal ministry a real matter of prayer, allowing God to reveal His place for you in ministry.

► Don't allow people to impose their gifts on you, and don't gravitate to, or colonize with, those who have the same gift as you.

► Don't be blind to others' gifts, but don't covet gifts God gave to someone else. He made no mistake when He gave your gift to you (see 1 Corinthians 12:18).

It's easy to fall into Satan's traps. He specializes in causing people to go to bad extremes over good things. Much of the guilt associated with Christian ministry is not conviction from the Holy Spirit but false guilt caused by not living up to the expectations of others.

DEAL WITH CONTROL ISSUES

As a church grows, the pastor's hands-on ministry must decrease, and the congregation's hands-on ministry must increase. This will be especially difficult for pastors who need to control. Top-down, oppressive, and dictatorial management is out in today's society. There is no room for a boss-pastor. A pastor's willingness to move to a team ministry is crucial to the effectiveness of a church's ministry.

Florence Littauer's well-known basic personality traits will factor into whether or not a pastor has control issues. Examine these traits, and honestly evaluate yourself.

Phlegmatic

The phlegmatic finds it easy to allow others to lead. Because of this, the phlegmatic sometimes needs to take more control than he or she actually wants.

Melancholic

The melancholic easily gets lost in mundane details and might "muddy the water" for team leaders.

Sanguine

The sanguine just wants to have fun. Life is a party! He or she wants everyone to be happy and has a tendency to be more interested in chatting and making friends than in actual leading.

Choleric

The choleric has a tendency to be bossy and finds it hard to let go of the reins. For example, this person may become a pastor-controller with the following characteristics.

The Pastor-Controller

1. Has a Lone Ranger mentality. "No one does it like me."
2. Limits decision-making to a small inner circle.
3. Is ego-centered. "No one cares for people like I do." For example, pastor-controllers rarely allow others to make hospital visits, because they gain affirmation from this type of ministry.
4. Pushes personal agendas.
5. Has a watchdog mentality that results in critical and negative behavior. Watches for mistakes rather than encouraging and serving as a resource.
6. Is inflexible with schedules, programs, innovations. "It's my way or the highway."

The remedy for the pastor-controller is to focus on becoming a pastor-coach who exhibits these characteristics:

1. Is willing to share in problem-solving, vision-casting, managing teams, and decision-making.
2. Develops guidelines of how teams will function.
3. Values giftedness in team members.
4. Keeps agreements.
5. Communicates the mission.
6. Is flexible.
7. Listens and understands team dynamics.
8. Makes the ministry people-oriented.
9. Uses the Word of God as a guide for ministry. (See Acts 6 as an example of giving up control and letting others serve.)
10. Helps Christians grow to maturity.

BUILDING TRUST

Sometimes a pastor finds it difficult to release control because of an issue with trust—and trust is a very important factor in cultivating effective teams. Charles Handy lists several principles of trust that will assist the pastor-controller with implementing Ministry Action Teams as a pastor-coach.[5]

Trust Is Not Blind

To trust people, we must know them. Take the time to develop relationships and bond with laypersons.

Trust Requires Learning

We must be open to new ideas for strengthening our teams. We should be discerning—knowing when to offer opinions and when not to.

Trust Is Tough

Gaining the trust of your congregation can take time and effort. Likewise, it takes time and effort to extend trust to individual laypersons. Pray that God will give you the strength to trust.

BEWARE OF EGO TRIPS

Ruth N. Koch and Kenneth C. Haugk tell of an incident in the career of former Dallas Cowboy head coach Tom Landry. He was lecturing his players after a game about their various antics after each touchdown. One had danced, another had wiggled, and still another had spiked the ball.

Landry said with a stern voice, "Act like you've been in the end zone before!" The coach wanted his players to be seen as competent team members, not individual hot shots.[6]

Nothing will destroy ministry teamwork faster than selfishness among team members. Several years ago, composer-performer Lionel Richie wrote and produced the popular song "We Are the World." He invited the luminaries of the music industry to cooperate on the record in order to raise money for starving people. On the day of the recording, he posted a sign next to the studio entrance that said, "Check your ego at the door." Richie's message was clear: The success of the record depends on everyone working together for a common purpose instead of merely promoting themselves.

Likewise, ministry team leaders need to understand that the defining moments in their lives may well occur in the context of a team victory rather than an individual accomplishment. Pat Riley, coach of the Miami Heat basketball team, once said, "My driving belief is that great teamwork is the only way to reach our ultimate moments, to create the breakthroughs that define our career, to fulfill our lives with a sense of lasting significance."

CREATING AN ATMOSPHERE OF AFFIRMATION

Palm trees don't grow in Alaska. It's too cold there. Tropical plants need warmth. Orchids don't bloom in the desert. It's too dry. Delicate flowers need plenty of moisture. If you want any plant to grow, you must provide the right atmosphere.

Obvious? Not always. Many leaders try to grow a team without providing the right climate. Team members need affirmation in order to thrive. Starve them for recognition, and they'll dry up faster than a tiger lily in Tunisia. But give them plenty of encouragement, and they'll grow as strong as sequoias and multiply like zucchinis.

Here's how to create an atmosphere of affirmation for your team.

Celebrate Success

You've been pushing for weeks on a big project. Team members exhausted themselves, but the big push paid off. Your big day came off without a hitch. Now it's over, right?

Not quite. As a leader, you have one more job to do: celebrate this success with the team.

Never let an achievement slip by unnoticed. When minor objectives are reached, call attention to them in staff meetings, or write e-mails of praise. When major goals are accomplished, have a blowout. Hold a party for the team, take the staff to dinner, or issue a bonus. When your team succeeds, celebrate.

Praise in Private

Set an example of affirmation by encouraging team members one to one. Make lavish use of cards, e-mails, or phone calls that say, "I appreciate you." Those "Atta boys" will not only encourage your volunteers but also set the standard for encouragement. Soon you'll notice staff members doing the same with their teammates and with you!

Praise in Public

You will teach encouragement when you praise teammates in front of each other. Let all team members know that their peers are making a valuable contribution. Show them that they should praise their teammates' success. Mention achievements at staff meetings. Affirm a teammate in the hearing of others. Be fair and evenhanded, no playing favorites; and beware of arousing envy. Simply let each team member know that you appreciate the contribution of the others.

Pay Attention to Team Needs and Progress

Your praise will ring hollow if it's not grounded in reality. Saying, "You're doing a great job," will be meaningless to a volunteer who knows that his work is struggling. Keep connected. Observe the achievements and failures of your team members, and offer encouragement accordingly. Asking "How can we learn together from this setback?" can be just as affirming as praising a success.

Don't forget to observe the personal success and struggles of your team. Remember birthdays. Ask about family life. Show an interest in their personal health. When team members know that you're tuned in to their needs, they'll have confidence in you as their leader.

Treat Paid Staff as if They Were Volunteers

Your paid staff are volunteers, you know. Every one of them could be making more money working somewhere else. They work for the church and for you because they believe in what they're doing. Give them the same positive reinforcement that you would give Sunday School teachers. Tell them that their work matters. Let them know you appreciate their presence and their contribution. They'll work harder; you'll look smarter.

Develop a Lifestyle of Affirmation

Are you an encourager? Some people aren't. Their pessimistic outlook on life spills into relationships. They dampen morale by dwelling on problems, never on praise.

Develop a personal style that promotes the success of others. Look team members in the eye, and listen to what they say. Ask how they are and what they need. Frequently say things like "I appreciate you," "Thank you," and "Good job." Your personal style will set the tone for your team.

▷ Team-building Tips

- ▸ Discover and develop the best talent you can.
- ▸ Give out rewards at the end of a team project.
- ▸ Lead by example.
- ▸ Emphasize the importance of disciplined work habits.
- ▸ Gain loyalty by making team members feel special.
- ▸ Mentor others, and you will multiply team effectiveness.
- ▸ Select leaders based on their commitment to Jesus Christ.
- ▸ Deal with team disagreement with discretion.
- ▸ Train team members to discover their spiritual gifts and unique personality traits.
- ▸ Emphasize team relationships, and de-emphasize rules.
- ▸ Model openness and caring.
- ▸ Recruit people for specific ministries.

▷ Resource Tip
Hiring the Right Staff

Staff members can make or break the ministry of a local church. While pastors are called upon to hire and manage staff—and recruit and direct volunteers—most receive little or no training in how to recruit, interview, select, and direct the work of others. For step-by-step help in all phases of this critical aspect of ministry, see *Stan Toler's Practical Guide to Hiring Staff*.

6

A MODEL OF MINISTRY ACTION TEAMS

WHEN THEY HAD PRAYED, THE PLACE WHERE THEY WERE
ASSEMBLED TOGETHER WAS SHAKEN; AND THEY WERE ALL
FILLED WITH THE HOLY SPIRIT, AND THEY SPOKE THE WORD OF
GOD WITH BOLDNESS. NOW THE MULTITUDE OF THOSE WHO
BELIEVED WERE OF ONE HEART AND ONE SOUL; NEITHER
DID ANYONE SAY THAT ANY OF THE THINGS HE POSSESSED
WAS HIS OWN, BUT THEY HAD ALL THINGS IN COMMON. AND
WITH GREAT POWER THE APOSTLES GAVE WITNESS TO THE
RESURRECTION OF THE LORD JESUS. AND GREAT GRACE WAS
UPON THEM ALL. NOR WAS THERE ANYONE AMONG THEM
WHO LACKED; FOR ALL WHO WERE POSSESSORS OF LANDS
OR HOUSES SOLD THEM, AND BROUGHT THE PROCEEDS
OF THE THINGS THAT WERE SOLD.

—ACTS 4:31–34

▲

Two men were riding a bicycle built for two. Everything seemed
to be going well until they started up a rather large hill, and then
the struggle ensued. When they reached the top, the man on the
first seat was gasping for breath. He looked back at his partner
and said, "That hill took a lot out of me!" The man in the second
seat said, "You're right—if I hadn't kept the brakes on all the way,
we would have rolled back down the hill!"

This delightful story gives us an insight into the church's ministry. When it comes to change, for instance, some people feel they are just doing their duty when they try to put the brakes on every bit of upward progress that is proposed.

> **MOST METHODS OF EVANGELISM THAT HAVE WORKED IN THE PAST ARE NOT WORKING TODAY.**
> —ALAN NELSON

My home church in Columbus, Ohio, closed several years ago. Just thirty years prior to that, the church thrived as one of the largest in the city. Its mistake? With community changes happening all around them, the church put the brakes on change in the church.

I visited the church nine months before it closed its doors. My parents stayed with the church until its final service. While I was there, I made several observations. For example, they continued in the same nonessential traditions without giving thought to what the rest of the church world was doing. They had a Sunday School, as many thriving churches do. But rather than update the program to match the times, they continued with the same Sunday School opening routine that was used when I was a teen, including singing the birthday song and handing out pencils. Nothing was innately wrong with any of their traditions—except that they seemed completely out of touch to people who were comparing that church with another church nearby that had fine-tuned its ministry to specifically target contemporary needs.

I am pleased that my home church never changed its belief in the Word of God, the sacraments of the Church, or the essentials of the faith. Those fundamentals must be our anchor in time of change. But neither did that church change its presentation of those foundational things. Putting the brakes on change became its downfall.

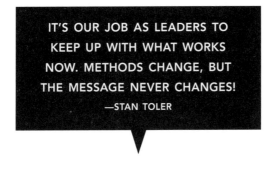

> IT'S OUR JOB AS LEADERS TO KEEP UP WITH WHAT WORKS NOW. METHODS CHANGE, BUT THE MESSAGE NEVER CHANGES!
> —STAN TOLER

NEW METHODS FOR A NEW DAY

Robert Kriegel wrote a book titled *If It Ain't Broke, Break It!* The target audience was corporate America. The book explored the concepts of working smarter and the idea of unleashing creative thought in the workforce. Certainly the Church can learn some things about cultural relevance from the marketplace. There are times when we need to break our nonessential tradition.

When I was trained to share my faith with others, we used the confrontational style of evangelism. Today, people don't respond to that style as readily as they do to the relationship method. Ministering in the twenty-first century calls for building relationship bridges to win souls. Trusting relationships are the key to reaching people for Christ and bonding them to His Church. Five specific characteristics denote whether something needs "breaking" in a church:

1. The church is focused on itself rather than the needs of the world around it.

2. There is perpetual conflict with church members standing opposite one another.

3. The people have no vision spiritually and no vision for the future of the church.

4. Membership has plateaued or is declining.

5. Facilities are unkempt. (An easy problem to remedy!)

Research done by church growth expert Win Arn shows that, as stated earlier, the more relationships an individual has within the church, the more apt that individual is to stay in the church. Conversely, the fewer relationships an individual has in the church, the less likely that individual will stay in the church. O. J. Bryson calls it *The Rule of Seven*. When a church member has seven close friends in a church, he or she is unlikely ever to leave it. As Elmer Towns says, "Relationship is the glue that makes people stick to the church."

Other research shows that eighty-six percent of those who accept Christ and join a church do so because of the influence of a friend or a relative—an existing relationship. In essence, the more relationships nonseekers have with those who attend church, the greater the chance they will become receptive to the gospel. Thus, if I want my unchurched friend to believe in Christ and attend my church, I must get my friend to establish a trusting relationship with as many of my churched friends as possible.

THE VISION

When I (Stan) accepted the pastorate of Trinity Church of the Nazarene in Oklahoma City, I inherited a church with an excellent sixty-three-year history, good pastors, and a track record of ministry success in the community.

I sought the Lord's guidance in building on that strength. Through research and counsel, I began to see the need for training leaders who would share the vision God had given me for the church. In the process, I discovered some workable ministry principles that enabled us to continue building a growing, healthy congregation.

PREPARATION IS THE KEY
TO GROWING THE CHURCH

Churches will not grow without preparing to grow. Churches don't "catch" growth like a cold; they make it a point to be farther ahead spiritually, financially, and numerically than they were previously. Preparation is important in any field of endeavor. Malcolm Fleschner writes,

> Preparation is part of the secret of the success of hockey superstar Wayne Gretzky. Gretzky is far and away the greatest hockey player of all time. On March 23, 1994, Gretzky scored his 802nd career goal, breaking the only important scoring record that remained out of his grasp. In all, Gretzky now holds more than 60 game, season, playoff and career scoring records. In the 1980s, Gretzky won the National Hockey League's Most Valuable Player award, an unprecedented nine of ten possible times. No athlete in any other sport in history comes close to this kind of domination over the record books. Gordie Howe, who owned the old goal-scoring record, needed 26 years to put that many pucks in the net. Gretzky did it in 15.
>
> But you wouldn't know it to look at him. He stands smaller than average for a hockey player—5'11"—and at 170 pounds weighs less than average too. He doesn't skate particularly fast or gracefully, his shot is not a real "burner," and on strength tests administered to each member of his team, Gretzky always placed dead last. So what makes the Great One so great?
>
> Gretzky credits his father with dozens of essential lessons, from practicing his stick handling in the off-season with a tennis ball (tennis balls are harder to control than pucks and teach you how to swat things out of the air) to attempting the unconventional.

"In practice," he says, "I try weird things like bouncing the puck off the side of the net to a teammate. I practiced it so much I can do it now in any direction. It's the same with the sideboards. People say there are only six men on the ice, but really, if you use the angle of deflection off the board, there are seven. If you count the net, that's eight. From the opening face-off, I always figure we have 'em, eight-on-six." Gretzky is the best-prepared member of his team.[6]

ELEVEN STEPS FOR GROWTH

During my first year as pastor of Trinity, we took some definite, preplanned steps toward casting a new vision. The following steps detail what our Ministry Vision Team did to move the church.

Step One: Town Hall Meeting

Every Sunday evening for four weeks we conducted "town hall meetings" in lieu of our Sunday evening service. Eleven team leaders were trained in small-group assessment and evaluation methods, asked to read Rick Warren's *The Purpose-Driven Church*, and given specific discussion quotas for each meeting. Additionally, the team leaders met each Wednesday evening and discussed what went on in their small-group meetings. Based on congregational feedback, we were prepared to move forward in ministry.

Step Two: Mission Statement

The Ministry Vision Team refined the mission statement of the church. Concern was given to include wording that reflected the Great Commission and the Great Commandment. Here is what we came up with:

Our mission is to make Christlike disciples in our city and in the nation.

Step Three: Vision Refinement

Next, a vision was implemented to extend our ministry into the twenty-first century. This vision was centered around the idea of *serving* and focused on the five "ships" that are at the heart of every local congregation.

We Envision Ourselves—

   S—eeking God

   E—xtending Grace

   R—eceiving Direction

   V—iewing the Future

   I—nvolving People

   N—urturing Life

   G—iving Generously

We Focus On—

Worship: Devoting ourselves to seeking God

Friendship: Extending God's grace to others (evangelism)

Discipleship: Growing together to become like Christ

Stewardship: Sharing through giving locally and globally

Partnership: Using our abilities to serve others

Step Four: Values Clarification

We then designed a values statement to hold us steady in a time of change.

Our Core Values

1. We value the souls of the lost (Luke 19:10).
2. We value personal integrity (Proverbs 10:9).
3. We value corporate worship (Hebrews 10:25).
4. We value the Word of God (Deuteronomy 6:6–9).
5. We value the gifts of God's people (Ephesians 4:11–13).
6. We value wholesome fellowship (1 John 1:7).
7. We value God's family (Psalm 133:1).

Step Five: Implement Ministry Action Teams

The committee system was completely overhauled to create Ministry Action Teams. Since every great team has a clear job description for its team members, as part of my organizational process at Trinity I met with every existing committee and chairperson and sought understanding as to the team's role in the church. With the help of Pastor Jeffrey Johnson, I then attempted to bring role definition and team understanding into sharp focus. The newly organized teams were empowered to act and to spend funds according to a present budget. They were released to do ministry based on our new vision plan. (Ministry Action Team descriptions are presented later in this chapter.)

Step Six: Focus on Inclusion

A welcome center was designed and built to meet the needs of our guests. Information packets were designed to share with our special visitors each Sunday.

Step Seven: Communication Widely

A Pastor's Welcome Class was started for the purpose of sharing our vision for reaching our community for Christ. We determined that our community needed to know not only that Trinity Church of the Nazarene was there but also *why* it was there.

Step Eight: Intentional Inclusion

Our Friendship Ministry Team began a pastor's brunch that followed the Sunday worship service every sixty days. All guests who attended during the previous two months were invited to have lunch with the pastoral staff and key lay leaders.

Step Nine: Discipleship Improvements

The Discipleship and Small Groups underwent some innovative changes. A Generation Excellence Class was added, as were additional special electives classes.

Step Ten: Leadership Training

Cultural and leadership training opportunities were offered. These were in the form of Lay Institute to Equip (LITE) and Strategic Advanced Leadership Training (SALT). These training opportunities began to move us toward becoming a learning organization.

Step Eleven: Worship Refinement

The traditional worship service received a facelift. The worship service included the blending of hymns and praise choruses into our worship.

Four Key Questions

During these important steps, we kept four key questions before the leaders of the ministry teams:

1. Who are we, and what are our beliefs and values?
2. What are our demographic possibilities for outreach?
3. If we believe we are living in the end times, are we willing to work like it?
4. Does this church belong to God or to an internal controlling faction?

THE MINISTRY VISION TEAM

Last, we began redefining the role of the church board. My first goal was to move us from dealing with small, inconsequential matters to become a vision-planning team. These statements helped us make that transition effectively.

Purpose of the Ministry Vision Team

It is the purpose of the Ministry Vision Team to give direction to the life and ministry of this church toward the accomplishment of the church's mission as stated by Christ. Accomplishing this purpose will involve—

Ministry. Developing and maintaining a strong, well-balanced, and inspirational church program that ministers to the needs of every age group so that all may grow and mature in discipleship.

Outreach. Developing and maintaining a definite program that involves our people in the outreach of the church. Doing so will require that we provide training, assistance, and direction as necessary for maximum effectiveness.

Facilities. Obtaining and maintaining facilities that are functional in nature, adequate in size, and equipped with sufficient equipment.

Finances. Developing and maintaining a program of financial support that is strong enough to underwrite these programs and facilities.

Organization of the Ministry Vision Team

To assure that positive attention is given to each of these areas, this team shall be organized as follows:

A total of sixteen team members (the church board) and three ex officio members.

The ex officio members are the missions team leader, youth team leader, and the Sunday School and Discipleship Ministries leader.

The team will elect officers from within the team by a ballot vote. These elected officers will serve as secretary and treasurer.

The board members will be appointed to serve in one of seven ministry teams. The five Ministry Action Teams are—

- ▸ Stewardship
- ▸ Worship

- Friendship
- Partnership
- Discipleship

The three auxiliary departments will be structured according to denominational requirements.

Team members are limited to a maximum of three consecutive one-year terms of service, after which they must rotate off the Ministry Vision Team for one year. It is expected that individuals leaving the team will be involved in subcommittee work. The three-year tenure includes the ex officio members.

Responsibilities of the Ministry Vision Team

The Ministry Vision Team will meet monthly to hear reports, review the minutes, conduct an annual audit, study statistics, review plans, and take appropriate action for the general operation of the church. Attendance at each monthly meeting is expected.

Resigning as the Chairman of the Board

One assignment I disliked the most as a pastor was serving as the chairman of the church board. I have never enjoyed chairing meetings. Frankly, I talk too much to be a chairman. Further, I tend to be thin-skinned when church board members are critical about a specific topic.

I finally resolved the matter by "resigning" as chairman of the board and appointing a qualified layperson in my place. Though I technically remained the chairman, I allowed my designee to function in my place. I came to realize that people were not criticizing me in the board meetings—they were merely trying to deal with areas of church ministry that needed help. They were the ones who cared enough to point out the problems. I then decided that a layperson chairing the meetings could take the heat better than I. To my surprise, I found that most board members were kinder and gentler to their peers.

With the new understanding that I didn't have to chair all the meetings or even be present for all the meetings (I did attend most meetings), I felt a great sense of release to do ministry. More than ever before, I was able to fulfill my best gifts.

I hasten to point out that I still had a vital role in the church board meeting, which we now called the Ministry Vision Team meeting. My role was to cast the vision. Therefore, I tried never to get caught up in mundane matters, realizing that my role was to lead the team to a new level of ministry.

The governmental structures for local churches in some denominations might prohibit pastors from allowing a layperson to chair the church board meeting. Pastors are well advised to seek the counsel of their supervisors before making a change in their church board structure.

Ministry Vision Team Leader

Now that I have mentioned the use of a board president, I would like to describe the role of this Ministry Vision Team leader. The following job description has been written for this important team leader at Trinity Church of the Nazarene. The Ministry Vision Team leader will perform the following duties.

Serve a specific term. Lead the Ministry Vision Team for a one-year term of service.

Assist the pastor. Serve as assistant to the pastor on the Executive Ministry Team.

Set the agenda. Prepare the agenda for the Ministry Vision Team meeting as a result of the Executive Ministry Team meeting, with the approval of the senior pastor and with consultation for additional action items.

Assume staff care. Assist the senior pastor in watch-care of the staff and their families.

Develop leadership. Spend top-quality time in encouragement of the team leaders and their various committees.

Assume legal responsibilities. Sign documents, checks, and other church papers as appropriate.

Following the meeting schedule. Call Ministry Vision Team meetings with the approval of the senior pastor, and/or the district superintendent in the absence of the senior pastor. No Ministry Vision Team meeting will be called without such approval.

Conduct meetings. Chair any specially called corporate officer meetings. Meetings are to be called with the approval of the senior pastor and whenever possible, at a time when the senior pastor can attend. The senior pastor is ex officio chairperson of all boards and committees of the local church.

Assume general leadership. Assist the pastor with the affairs and activities of the church, with love and loyalty for all.

MINISTRY ACTION TEAM DESCRIPTIONS

After establishing a team leader for the church board, the next important issue was the employment of Ministry Action Teams and leaders. One team was created for each of the five "ships" that were mentioned earlier.

Leaders

After many meetings in the study committees at Trinity, we were able to develop the following job description for our team leaders.

Appointment and Term. Ministry Action Team leaders will be appointed by the pastor. This appointment will be for a one-year term of service. Ministry Action Team leaders can be appointed for more than one year, but they cannot lead the same team for two consecutive years. This does not include the Stewardship Ministry Action Team.

Reporting. Each team leader will make a monthly report to the Executive Ministry Team and to the Ministry Vision Team.

Spending Approval. Each team leader is responsible for submitting to the Executive Ministry Team any expenditure that needs additional approval.

Agenda Creation. Monthly committee information submitted by the team leaders will form the completed agenda for the next Ministry Vision Team meeting.

Team Meetings. Team leaders should meet monthly with their teammates. They should never conduct a meaningless meeting—meetings should be canceled if there is no reason for them.

Teams

Every leader needs a team. The following clarify the expectations I established for the Ministry Action Teams.

Membership. Each team will consist of a leader and at least two members.

Meetings. Each team is expected to meet once a month. The leader is responsible for communicating the time, date, and place of each meeting.

Finances. Each team will have financial guidelines, recommended by the Stewardship Ministry Action Team and ratified by the Ministry Vision Team, that entitles each team to make financial decisions independent of Ministry Vision Team approval. Each team will have a financial ceiling cap that will require certain expenditures to be approved by the Executive Ministry Team.

Structure. The auxiliary committees—youth, missions, and Sunday School—are to be structured according to *Manual* requirements. Each of these auxiliary presidents and superintendents will be assigned a Ministry Action Team leader to assist him or her in ministry when needed.

Involvement. The goal is involvement. Measure the success of events by the number of people you involve in the process. Each team is responsible to involve non-board members and church attendees to serve on ministry teams.

MINISTRY ACTION TEAM MODEL

Since I have been discussing ministry in general terms, the following example of our Partnership Ministry Action Team may provide additional insight and offer a guideline for the teams you choose to develop.

Team Purpose

The purpose of the Partnership Ministry Team is to direct the maintenance, improvement, and development of all church properties and equipment to assure adequate and functional facilities to meet the needs of the total program and growth of the local church under the Partnership Ministry Action Team.

Guiding Question

How can we equip and maintain our total facilities to provide the best possible environment for our local ministries?

Team Responsibilities

1. To provide for maintenance and improvements of all church-owned buildings, keeping them in attractive and functional condition at all times.

2. To provide for maintenance and improvement of all grounds, grass, and shrubbery, to supervise landscape improvements, and to secure snow and ice removal when necessary.

3. To provide for care and maintenance of all church-owned equipment and vehicles and to keep a current inventory of them.

4. To recommend, for Ministry Vision Team approval, policy for the use of all facilities and equipment and to provide for periodic review of existing policy to assure appropriate updating or changing.

5. To supervise the work of all custodial personnel.

6. To provide for and maintain the security of the church building.

7. To anticipate need for additional equipment and to recommend, for Monthly Vision Team approval, the acquisition of additional equipment when needed.

8. To provide for adequate insurance coverage for the church.

9. To prepare an asking budget and to present it to the Executive Ministry Team in preparation of the annual church budget.

MINISTRY TEAM LEADER MODEL

Every team needs a leader, and defining the responsibilities of that leader is crucial for the team's success. Here is a model ministry description for the leader of the Partnership Ministry Action Team.

Purpose

To oversee the involvement of many people in the maintenance, improvement, and development of all church properties and equipment to assure adequate functional facilities to meet the needs of the total program and growth of Trinity Church of the Nazarene.

Function

To encourage, recruit, and appoint the necessary personnel to provide for the best possible environment for the ministries of Trinity Church of the Nazarene.

Responsibilities

1. Conduct monthly Buildings and Properties Ministry Team meetings and report to the Ministry Vision Team.

2. Appoint leaders for these ministry areas:

▸ Maintenance

- Security
- Equipment
- Motor Vehicles
- Facilities Insurance/Policy/Custodial Supervision
- Property Improvements
- Office Equipment
- Lay Ministry Fair

2. Oversee the financial planning and stewardship in the areas of ministry encompassed by this team.

3. Coordinate planning in the areas of ministry encompassed by this team, in cooperation with the pastoral staff.

4. Meet monthly with the Executive Ministry Team.

THE ROLE OF PASTORAL STAFF

So where does the paid staff fit into all of this? The answer is simple: They are part of the church ministry team and must learn to work with Ministry Action Team leaders. There's no room for Lone Ranger types on the team. Every staff member matches up with a team leader and is asked to resource and encourage the lay ministers with whom they work. The following job description for the pastoral team has provided guidance for the paid leadership team at Trinity.

Pastoral Staff Member Expectations

The senior pastor and staff will meet weekly in a regular session to deal with spiritual and administrative matters of the church.

The staff will work with the appropriate Ministry Action Team leaders to facilitate their individual ministries.

The Executive Ministry Team and Ministry Action Teams are to work with the staff to facilitate the ministries of the staff as well.

The staff will make any financial request that needs additional approval to their Ministry Action Team leader.

The team leader is responsible for taking this matter to the appropriate team, or the Executive Ministry Team, if needed.

The pastor maintains full responsibility for the staff and their own individual ministries. The Ministry Action Team leaders' involvement does not override the pastor's responsibility for the staff.

The Model Team

It is crucial for paid staff members to model teamwork and accountability for the lay ministry teams. The design of the above ministry description reflected our desire to work together with the church team leaders at Trinity. Our "ships"—worship, friendship, discipleship, stewardship, partnership—sailed smoothly when our ministry teammates had clearly defined roles and job descriptions. Empowered leaders with a clear understanding of their ministry assignments assist greatly in Kingdom-building!

We must welcome the future, remembering that soon it will be the past; and we must respect the past, remembering that it was once all that was humanly possible.

—George Santayana

A FINAL WORD: STICK TOGETHER

Perhaps you've heard about the troop of Boy Scouts who gathered for the annual hike in the woods. Taking off at sunrise, they commenced a fifteen-mile trek through some of the most scenic grounds in the country. About midmorning, they came across an abandoned section of railroad track. Each in turn tried to walk the narrow rails, but after only a few unsteady steps, each lost his balance and tumbled off.

After watching one after another fall off the iron rail, two of the boys offered a bet to the rest of the troop. The two bet that they could both walk the entire length of the railroad track without falling off even once.

The other boys laughed and said, "No way!" Challenged to make good their boast, the two boys jumped up onto opposite rails, simply reached out and held hands to balance each other, and steadily walked the entire section of track with no difficulty.

The moral of the story is that seemingly impossible tasks are easier when we are willing to work together. To keep from stumbling, we need to reach out to our teammates and never quit holding hands.

I realize that some of you will be implementing these changes within the context of a small- or medium-sized church, and the task might seem impossible. But don't despair. I've been there, and I've learned that the best method is to gradually begin to make the changes you can make. The other changes will come in time. Even if you can initially establish only three Ministry Action Teams, grab the hands of your gifted laypersons—and begin walking down that track.

▷ **Team-building Tips**

- ▸ Ask for feedback to be directed to the entire team.
- ▸ Take the entire team to a leadership seminar.
- ▸ Build an atmosphere that is conducive to open communication.
- ▸ Remember that team members will sometimes fail.
- ▸ Teach the team Ephesians 4:11–12.
- ▸ Resign as general manager of the universe, and let God guide the team

▷ **Resource Tip**
Creating Effective Policies and Procedures

Smooth operation of a local church doesn't just happen. It flows from carefully designed processes. Drafting strong policies, procedures, and, yes, even forms is critical for keeping ministry teams—and other aspects of church life—functioning as they should. For a complete guide to the smooth operation of a local church ministry, including sample purpose statements, policies, and forms, see *Church Operations Manual: A Step-by-Step Guide to Effective Church Management,* by Stan Toler.

ABOUT THE AUTHORS

▲

Stan Toler is a general superintendent in the Church of the Nazarene. He previously served for forty years as a pastor in Ohio, Florida, Tennessee, and Oklahoma. Dr. Toler has written more than eighty books, including his best-sellers:

- *God Has Never Failed Me, but He's Sure Scared Me to Death a Few Times*
- *The Buzzards Are Circling, but God's Not Finished With Me Yet*
- *God Is Never Late; He's Seldom Early; He's Always Right on Time*
- *The Secret Blend*
- *Secrets of Becoming the Richest Person in the World*
- *Practical Guide to Pastoral Ministry*
- *The Inspirational Speaker's Resource*
- *ReThink Your Life*
- The *Minute Motivators* series
- *If Only I Could Relate to the People I'm Related To*
- *The Pastor's Wedding Planner*
- *The Pastor's Funeral Planner*

For many years he served as vice-president for John C. Maxwell's Leadership Institute, teaching seminars and training church and corporate leaders to make a difference in the world. He and his wife, Linda, an educator, have two married sons and two grandsons

Larry Gilbert is founder and CEO of Ephesians Four Ministries, the parent corporation of Church Growth Institute, which has published his numerous resources on spiritual-gifts-based team ministry. To date, his best-selling *Team Ministry Spiritual Gifts Inventory* has helped almost five million people discover their dominant spiritual gifts. Dr. Gilbert and his wife, Mary Lou, live in Elkton, Maryland.

NOTES

▲

Chapter 1

1. Ronald E. Merrill and Henry D. Sedgwick, *INC* magazine, August 1994.

2. R. Daniel Reeves, *Ministry Advantage* 8, No. 1.

3. *The MacIntosh Growth Network Newsletter,* December 1998.

Chapter 3

1. *Pastor's Family,* February-March, 1997.

2. J. Winston Pearce, *Planning Your Preaching* (Nashville: Broadman Press, 1987).

3. Peter Drucker, *The Effective Executive* (New York: Harper & Row, 1966), 75.

4. James B. Miller, *The Corporate Coach* (New York: Harper Collins Publishing, 1993), 126–27.

Chapter 4

1. Marlene Wilson, "Turning Pewsitters into Players," *Leadership Journal*, fall 1996.

2. Robert B. Maddux, *Team Building: An Exercise in Leadership* (Los Altos, Calif.: Crisp Publishing, 1992), 11.

3. Chris Russell "Effective Delegation," *Today's Christian Preacher*, summer 1997).

4. John C. Maxwell, *Developing the Leaders Around You* (Nashville: Thomas Nelson Publishers, 1995), 9.

5. Og Mandino, *Og Mandino's University of Success* (New York: Bantam Books, 1982).

Chapter 5

1. Glenn M. Parker, *Team Players and Teamwork* (San Francisco: Jossey-Bass Publishers, 1996), 81.

2. *Bottom Line*, vol. 1, no. 3.

3. Maddux, *Team Building*, 19.

4. Adapted from Tim Radlaff, *CopyFast Print Shop Newsletter*, 1999.

5. Charles Handy, *The Hungry Spirit: Beyond Capitalism, A Quest for Purpose in the Modern World* (New York: Broadway Books, 1999).

6. Ruth N. Koch and Kenneth C. Haugk, *Speaking the Truth in Love* (St. Louis: Stephen Ministries, 1992).

Chapter 6

1. Malcolm Fleschner, "Take Your Best Shot," *Personal Selling Power* (July-August, 1994), 72.

OTHER BOOKS BY STAN TOLER . . .

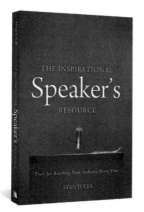

Stan Toler shares proven methods and tips to help you overcome your fear of public speaking and convey your ideas clearly and persuasively. An invaluable tool for achieving public-speaking success.

Expanding your vision, this book, provides practical, satisfying insight that will challenge your understanding of greatness and motivate you to be an effective, devoted servant who leads from last place.

If you want to be a great leader, authentic and faithful in all you do, then begin by following the wisdom and models given to you through this glimpse into the Book of Psalms.

Learning to Be Last
By E. Lebron Fairbanks & Stan Toler
ISBN: 978-0-8341-2353-3

Maximum Integrity
By Stan Toler & Jerry Brecheisen
ISBN: 978-0-8341-2283-3

The Inspirational Speaker's Resource
By Stan Toler
ISBN: 978-0-8341-2449-3

BEACON HILL PRESS
OF KANSAS CITY

Available online at BeaconHillBooks.com